THE
ORIGINAL
GHOSTS
OF THE
Isle of Wight

D1134021

GAY BALDWIN

New edition updated and revised
Copyright © Gay Baldwin 1997

Original Copyright Steedman and Anker 1977
First published in December 1977
Second reprint, February 1978
Third reprint, August 1981
Fourth reprint, May 1987
Fifth reprint, March 1992

Published by Gay Baldwin
9 Pine Tree Close,
Cowes,
Isle of Wight
PO31 8DX
England

Distributed by Gay Baldwin
Telephone (01983) 294651

Text set by IW Council Print Unit.
Printed by Short Run Press, Exeter.

ISBN 0-9520062-4-3

CONTENTS

INTRODUCTION

I spent a couple of weeks exploring the hauntings of the Isle of Wight back in 1980, but Gay Baldwin has produced no less than four books on the Island ghosts and she is without doubt the authority on ghosts and ghostly activity on the Isle of Wight.

Presenting each case carefully and drawing on original research there is a wealth of detail presented in a readable style and whether you are an armchair investigator or a field worker in this fascinating realm, "Ghosts of the Isle of Wight" is essential reading.

It gives me great pleasure to recommend a book that has a treasured place in my library and an author who always looks for a natural explanation before considering a supernatural one, and an author who can make the most frightening ghost sound attractive - at least to a fellow ghost hunter!

Peter Underwood FRSA
President: The Ghost Club Society

WHAT IS A GHOST?

"All houses in which men have lived and died
Are haunted houses: through open doors
The harmless phantoms on their errands glide
With feet that make no sound upon the floors"

Longfellow

Ghosts of the Isle of Wight has come of age at last. Originally published in 1977, this first-ever collection of genuine Island ghost stories has become a local classic - and definitive reading for anyone interested in the supernatural side of the Isle of Wight. Copies of the little book with its familiar black cover can be found in many Island homes where it is still essential bedtime reading for generations of local schoolchildren.

Incredibly, this original Ghosts of the Isle of Wight has since inspired a series of sequels, a video of haunted places and interviews with some of those featured in the books, and the Newport Ghostwalk, an historical walk through the old town's dark past.

Far from diminishing, interest in the paranormal seems to increase with the years. People today are far more willing to keep an open mind about the possibility that ghosts might and do exist.

So what is a ghost? Theories abound. A ghost is mere illusion, over-active imagination, rats in the attic, wishful thinking......some say. To others a ghost is an unexplained physical disturbance in the brain's interpretation of the frequencies of light, or a subjective hallucination communicated telepathically to others. It's a mental picture created under such stress or powerful emotion that it survives the death of the creator, awaiting the right receptive receiver. It's a compression of psychons or mind matter, left behind as a man might leave a widow or a will. It's the restless, discarnate spirit or soul of the dead.

Does man's undying mind carry a charge of energy which, after death, can become part of the energy pattern of its surroundings, a room or lonely lane? Does a haunted house have its own memories? Do ghosts walk when there is no-one there to see or hear them? Do they need to draw on our energy fields in order to materialise, so that we feel a cold shiver when they are around?

There are so many unanswered questions and although I have been investigating stories and researching the subject for many years, I have some theories but no real answers. One thing is certain however, the world is not as it seems.

Since this book was first written, people have moved on ....and in some cases passed on. Houses have changed hands, often several times in the intervening years. I have re-visited most of the haunted locations to discover whether the ghosts are still active. In most cases they are!

Some stories have been discarded, others updated and new ones added. I and many thousands of readers owe a debt of gratitude to those brave souls who overcame fear of ridicule all those years ago and allowed their stories to be told. Many have become an established part of Island ghost-lore and have helped to bring an acceptance and almost respectability to the idea of ghosts.

But most of all I want to thank Ray Anker, my original co-author and mentor, without whom Ghosts of the Isle of Wight would never have seen the light of day - and the darker side of the Isle of Wight would have gone unrecorded. Ghost-hunting in some of those little country pubs was hard work .... but someone had to do it!

"Do I believe in ghosts? No, but I am afraid of them."
(Marie Anne, Marquise du Deffand, 1697-1780)

Chapter One

HAUNTING TALES OF NEWPORT

DUEL TO THE DEATH....

Their pistols primed and ready, the two officers took aim and fired. Two shots rang out. Only one found its mark. The seconds ran to the wounded man who was bleeding heavily from the right shoulder. A servant was hastily sent for a surgeon. He could do little, for the shot had torn through lung and spinal cord.

For two long days the unfortunate man, Lieutenant John Blundell of the 101st Regiment, lay in agony on his deathbed at the Wheatsheaf Hotel in Newport's St Thomas's Square. He breathed his last on Sunday, 11th July 1813, and was buried at Church Litten graveyard, nearby, two days later. He was just 28 years old. Anne, his distraught young bride, could not believe her dashing lieutenant husband of just a few days, was dead - because of a petty quarrel over a coat he had borrowed from a brother officer, Lieutenant Maguire, to wear at the wedding.

The argument grew more bitter, urged on by fellow officers, his so-called friends. It became a matter of honour. Neither man would back down. It could only be settled by a duel. The challenge was made, albeit reluctantly, by Lieutenant Blundell.

The country was at war with Napoleon's France, and to prevent any invasion of the Island, considered a vital strategic point, several regiments were stationed in Niton village, at what is now Barrack Shute. When news of the proposed duel reached local clergyman and JP, the Reverend James Barwis, he hurried to the officers' mess to try to prevent it taking place. But feelings were running too high. By now the very honour of the regiment was at stake, and although neither man was frankly keen to fight, their fellow officers insisted the duel must take place.

In deference to the vicar's feelings they gave their word that no duel would be fought in the parish of Niton. Arrangements were made instead for the confrontation to take place just outside the walls of Carisbrooke Castle at dawn on Friday, July 9. Reverend Barwis appeared to have been satisfied with this. Eye witness accounts from both the inquest and subsequent murder trial show that the opposing parties met under the eastern wall of the castle, adjacent to the bowling green, in the dry ditch which runs parallel to the walls. A spot considered ideal for a duel, as neither man would have any advantage from the right.

Lieutenant Gilchrist was Blundell's second, while Lieutenant Hemming undertook the same duty for Maguire. Two other officers of the regiment, Kingsley and Slater, were also present.

PISTOLS AT THE READY

The pistols were chosen, examined, carefully primed and loaded. The men shook hands, then as the number of paces was counted out, both turned to fire. Shots were exchanged without hitting their target and Blundell's pistol burst. He borrowed one of Maguire's pistols, then both men took aim and fired again.

Blundell's shot went wide, but Maguire's bullet struck him in the shoulder. He fell to the ground, blood pumping from the jagged wound. Gilchrist sent his servant to fetch a surgeon, but before help arrived, Maguire and the seconds made themselves scarce. Those officers who remained said that after Blundell fell, he shook hands with Maguire and forgave him.

Attended by the regimental surgeon, Blundell was taken to a bedroom at the Wheatsheaf Hotel. The gravity of his wound was apparent; if he survived it would be a miracle. The dying man told Captain T. Baylis of the Army depot staff that he had fought Maguire against his own wishes. It was some of the officers of his regiment who had insisted he should fight.

Blundell's new father-in-law, Mr Henry White of Niton, visited him at the hotel the next day. The young officer on his deathbed, said it was a "bad business". He could barely speak, but was bitter that no attempt had been made to reconcile the matter. He had not wanted to fight but had been forced to by other officers, he said. Hours later he was dead. At the inquest held by Isle of Wight Coroner, Thomas Sewell, post mortem evidence showed that the bullet had penetrated Blundell's right shoulder blade, passed through his left lung injuring the spinal marrow and breaking the sixth rib, and embedding itself under the left arm-pit.

A verdict of wilful murder was returned by the inquest jury, and Maguire, the seconds Dill, Gilchrist, and Ensign O'Brien - apparently

The haunted Wheatsheaf Hotel at Newport

one of the main instigators - were duly charged. When they appeared before Mr Justice Gibbs at Winchester Assizes on 31st July 1813, there was virtually no evidence for the defence. Maguire told the court he had been challenged by the deceased, and, as a officer and gentleman, had been bound to fight.

The judge, clearly unimpressed by this argument, placed the black cap on his head to pronounce the death sentence upon all four defendants. In scathing tones, he said that the duel had been fought over a trivial cause. Not only had no attempt been made to reconcile the parties by brother officers, but on the contrary, "great pains had been taken, most unwarrantedly, to instigate and promote the fatal meeting."

After several postponements of the sentence, all four men were eventually pardoned by the Prince Regent. Following this, the Commander-in-Chief of the Army ordered a military inquiry. He concluded that, "of all the parties concerned, the unfortunate officer who lost his life, and the yet more unfortunate one by whose hand his comrade fell, were the least culpable." He proceeded to single out for special censure Lieutenants Dillon, Gilchrist and Ensign O'Brien, and threw them out of the Army, declaring them to be no longer officers in His Majesty's Service.

So ended one of the last duels to be fought on the Isle of Wight - the last is believed to have taken place at Northwood Park, Cowes, after a quarrel over a card game. The headstone of the loser, 22-year-old John Sutton, killed on 16th December, 1817, can still be seen at St Mary's churchyard, nearby.

A TRAGIC YOUNG WIDOW

But that is not the end of the story by any means. What of Lieutenant Blundell's young bride, Anne? The couple were married but a few short days before she was widowed - for a second time! Just 18-years-old when she wed John Blundell, Anne was already a widow when she met him at Niton. Her first husband was an officer at Portsmouth. The couple met when she went down to the sea to bathe, and when her father refused his consent to their marriage, they eloped to London. Five weeks later his regiment was ordered to Portugal, where he was one of the first to be killed in action. His young bride, now reconciled with her family, accompanied her mother to their holiday home at Niton. There she met and swiftly married Lieutenant Blundell. He, however, was so poor that he had to borrow a coat to be married in from Maguire, his brother officer.

Little more is known of the luckless Anne, just eighteen and already twice widowed. No mention is made of her in the inquest or trial records. However, for some years afterwards on the anniversary of his death, the initials J.B. were cut into the turf at the spot where John Blundell fell, and a posy of flowers was laid there. Locals believe it was Anne who made a pilgrimage to the castle every year until they were re-united in death.

So is it her ghost which haunts that bedroom at the Wheatsheaf Hotel, in which the unfortunate lieutenant died? The shade of a young woman has been seen sitting on the bed in that first floor room. One guest refused to sleep there and asked for another room after he felt the ghostly figure sitting on the end of his bed. Undeterred by this experience, he returned to the Wheatsheaf some months later, but insisted he did not want that original room again. "I really don't believe in ghosts, but there is something in that room, and I don't want to meet it again," he told staff. Could that poignant presence be the young bride who grieves still at her Lieutenant's death-bed long after that senseless and tragic duel?

WHERE A LOST SOUL SEEKS A BODY

The pastor gave a solemn warning: a soul which had not found rest might try to enter a living body to escape from its travail in the after-life. To protect herself, his companion hung a small gold cross round her neck. He clasped a Bible.

Together as midnight came they walked into the haunted building. They waited. The lights were on. All was quiet. And then both had a feeling that they were no longer alone. Something else was there. Something that was coming towards them. The pastor opened his Bible and read it aloud. The woman fingered her crucifix. But the presence they could feel, yet could not see, came on. They took one look at each other and made a dash for the door ....

This is fact, not fiction. It is no Gothic ghost story set in some brooding, ivy-covered hall. It happened in 1976 in what was soon to be a bright and busy store in Newport High Street. By day the "Handiyman" DIY Store, later the Sainsbury Homecare Store, was filled with do-it-your-selfers. By night something else walked there. It was never actually seen, but often made its presence felt. In previous years when Borough Hall garage and its workshops occupied the site, night staff would speak of eerie experiences. These grew eerier still when work began on extending the original DIY store premises in Pyle Street and converting the garage into a new High Street outlet. Workmen soon found they had disturbed more than brick and plaster.

In the early months of 1976, men employed by a mainland contractor to carry out the alterations slept in camp beds on the premises. They found themselves being woken by the sound of footsteps, though but for them, the place was deserted. More than once, they woke to hear the side doors sliding open and footsteps crossing the floor of the big empty building. Doors on the opposite wall would bang and rattle as if being opened by invisible hands, yet they could see nothing. After the first week they travelled to and from the Island every day rather than spend another night there.

Others came in to lay a new floor. It was a big job and they worked throughout the night. This time something was seen. Polythene sheeting laid on the floor moved oddly in a manner which could not be explained by draughts - more as if an unseen entity was walking across it. At about 3am in the presence of two startled workers and an onlooking policeman, an unused hosepipe suddenly rose from the ground and in the words of Handiyman manager Ray Pearson "leaped around."

It was Ray's wife, Audrey, who accompanied an Island minister on that brief attempt at ridding the building of its ghost. Their visit followed the workmen's complaints and, as a manageress, Audrey decided to find out for herself what was wrong. The minister, who now lives in Warwickshire, then pastor of an East Wight congregation, preferred to say nothing about events that night. But he was in no doubt that something extraordinary had occurred. Audrey Pearson was certain of that too. Whatever power was there was not visible or tangible, there was neither the odour nor the icy chill often associated with such experiences. There was simply the overwhelming feeling that something awful was drawing closer and closer.

Someone who remembered how genuinely alarmed they were was Sue Bennett, of Winston Road, Newport. A friend of the pastor, she was waiting outside the store in her car. She described how they suddenly ran out, obviously frightened. She herself firmly refused to set foot inside the door.

In the daytime the store is a spacious, airy building which would seem the last place in which to meet a ghost. Nevertheless, as night fell the atmosphere changed. Neither Ray nor Audrey Pearson cared to stay there too late. Odd things happened. For example, Ray found himself locked, late one night, behind a fire door which simply could not be locked. "When I did get out, I ran," he said. "I admit it, I was scared."

What lies behind the haunting of that store? One theory is that the restless soul which worried the pastor is that of a dead driver taken to the garage in the wreck of his crashed car. But it must be remembered that this is a very old part of Newport. Ancient cottages once stood here, their history now forgotten. Perhaps whatever walked a modern store by night walked out of a different age.

Over the years since this story was written, various staff at the DIY store have told me of curious happenings which still go on there. Footsteps are heard late at night, when the building is locked and empty. Things are moved in the showroom and when staff arrive some mornings, they discover tins or packets lying opened on the floor. They simply could not have fallen off the shelves. The haunting continues......

HAUNTED HAZARDS HOUSE

Almost opposite the DIY store once stood Hazards House, a fine old 17th century building now gone, along with other venerable properties such as the Swan Hotel, to make way for County Hall. It had to go - apart from planning needs, the house was in danger of collapse. Gone too is its ghost - although County Hall itself is haunted by other restless spirits. (Read about the ghost with a briefcase who frightened cleaners in *More Ghosts of the IW* and about the mischievous spirit on the fifth floor in *IW Ghosts Book Four*).

Hazards House was so named because it was built on what was then hazardous land near the river. One of the oldest private houses in Newport, it was re-built in 1684. Hazards House was once a girls' school run by the three Victorian sisters, the Misses Nicholson.

Phantom footsteps were heard, and a Newport businesswoman working there actually apologised to an apparition. Miss Audrey Spanner, who with her brother ran the century-old High Street drapery business which bore their name, was an air-raid warden during the last war. The ARP report centre was in the cellars of Hazards House. Miss Spanner, about to go down there from the top landing one day, suddenly had to step aside as someone was in her way.

"I started, and said, 'I beg your pardon'. Then I saw the figure disappear somewhere down by the wall. It was a shadowy form but I definitely saw it and I believe it was female - it seemed to be wearing a long skirt. But it didn't frighten me."

Miss Spanner thought it best to say nothing when she returned to the

County Hall now stands on the site of Hazards House

report centre, but next day mentioned her strange meeting to Eileen Cooper, whose post was also in the old house. Together they went up to the landing. There, where the figure had disappeared, they found an old back staircase which had been bricked up.

The late Miss Cooper, a former Registrar of Deaths and Marriages, spent many years in local Government service. Like Miss Spanner she was an impressive witness and left the pruning of her roses to talk about the Hazards House ghost with some reluctance. "More than once those of us at Hazards House felt something brush past us. Quite a lot of people felt it. It was just a touch, a gossamer touch as they say, as if from a very light curtain. There was a definite feeling of a presence at times. We played it down, of course - there were a lot of other things to think about during the war. But it was generally accepted that Hazards House was haunted."

No-one knows the origin of the haunting, but it was said that the vanished house contained "a nasty dark cupboard" in which a maidservant killed herself long ago.

WATCHER IN THE DARK

On the other side of the High Street there are reports of strange feelings and a phantom cat. John Hacker lives with his wife Susan in a period cottage next to the Unitarian Meeting House, where he is caretaker. Like everyone else, John finds the hall pleasant enough in daylight and, for that matter, in the evening. It's late at night when he walks through the 18th century building in the dark to switch on the lights from the rear, that he gets a feeling he is being watched.

"It's a feeling that there is someone or something behind me - quite a strong feeling," he said. "Then it almost seems as if something comes floating down from the balcony - I can't describe it. Once I thought I heard a voice chuckling in the darkness...." He's not frightened. He simply turns round and switches on his torch. There's nothing there - except for a "cold spot" which is almost tangible. But Susan Hacker is alarmed by the atmosphere she feels in the meeting house at night. She won't go into the building by herself.

The couple's cottage is haunted by a cat. John caught a glimpse of it once when he looked up from the book he was reading in bed, but usually it is felt on people's laps. There's a sudden feeling of cold, no real

sense of weight, and then the steady, repetitive kneading of paws which any cat-owner will recognise. The couple's dog, Sam the Labrador, saw it once. He stared at something no-one else could see. His hair stood up, he jumped on a chair and he would not come down until it had gone.

Is there a watcher in the dark at the Unitarian Meeting House?

THE MAUVE LADY OF LUGLEY STREET

When walking in Newport, look out for the Mauve Lady of Lugley Street, who has been seen countless times over the years. As a boy, Trevor Evans and his family lived at Number 68, in a house now used as offices by solicitors Roach Pittis. His sisters Josie and Daphne shared a bedroom. In that room both saw the figure of a woman in a mauve crinoline dress float noiselessly across the floor and disappear through a wardrobe. They never saw it at the same time. It was only after several individual sightings that they finally admitted what they had seen to each other. Not a detail differed.

This singularly tranquil and beautiful phantom was also seen, late one summer evening in 1971, by two American visitors. There was a sudden thunderstorm. In torrential rain they crouched in the inadequate shelter of a doorway to 54 Lugley Street. They noticed a woman in a long, dark cloak which covered a mauve gown coming across the road towards them. Commenting on the downpour, they said to her, "What awful weather this is."

The woman replied, "Aye" in apparent agreement, and walked past them.....straight through the solid wooden door!

THE OXFAM SHOP GHOST

Just across the road is the town's Oxfam shop, where a little old man in a three-cornered hat peeped at a small boy in bed, then smiled before he vanished.

Trevor Evans' family moved there before the last war, when his father ran a furniture shop on the ground floor. Odd things occurred. His mother often saw the handle on a parlour door turn of its own accord. The door would open. There would be no-one there. Then the door would shut itself. Lying awake in bed as a boy, Trevor would hear footsteps mounting the stairs when no-one was present. Then one night that little man in the 18th century hat appeared. "He looked at me, nodded, and smiled," said Trevor, now retired from the RNLI, who recalls that moment vividly. "I screamed."

On the first floor landing of the house, situated on the corner of Lugley Street and Lower St James' Street, was a spot that was always cold. Trevor's sister was in the hall saying goodnight to a boyfriend, when both of them felt something "swish" downstairs and past them.

The ground floor is now occupied by an Oxfam shop, a cheerful, friendly place haunted only by customers in search of a bargain. No ghosts here. But do they still walk in the higher reaches of the four-storey Georgian building? Oxfam's mainland organisation gave me and a companion permission to see for ourselves. We spent three hours there through midnight, wandering along dusty passageways, waiting in long-disused attics where moonlight and street lamp threw ragged shadows on the walls. Inevitably the rambling old house had a certain atmosphere which some might have regarded as eerie. We can report only three small, curious happenings.

At precisely 11.40pm, at the top of a flight of stairs above the shop, the temperature appeared to drop perceptibly, yet no fall was registered on our thermometer. The chill lasted for half a minute. Midnight came and went in quietness. At 12.15am the chill returned, this time on a higher landing. Again it lasted for half a minute. There were no draughts. The night was warm. The feeling came and went abruptly.

The other incident occurred at 1am. Behind us in the darkness something moved. We flicked on a torch to see the door to an attic staircase slowly swing open. We were relieved, and perhaps a trifle disappointed, that no little man in a tricorn hat stood there smiling in the thin torch beam. What we did find strange was that the old door had moved against its natural momentum. Unless pushed it would swing only in the opposite direction as if to close itself. We tried a dozen times to start it swinging open by itself. We didn't succeed.

What caused these cold spells and a door's peculiar behaviour - imagination or cooling timbers perhaps? We felt nothing menacing. The building itself is believed to stand near the site of the old town gibbet. Could this have any bearing on the haunting here? Perhaps the good work going on below has laid the ghost. Perhaps, as we were hunting him, he was further along Lugley Street paying court to that lovely Mauve Lady.

In 1996 the building suffered structural problems and while extensive repairs were carried out, the Oxfam shop moved for a time to premises nearby. Once the shop re-opened I asked the volunteer staff if the ghost had been upset by all the renovation work.

"No, it's all been quiet," they assured me. However, one confided, "A couple of years ago I was upstairs in one of the front rooms when suddenly the temperature dropped about ten degrees. The room became icy cold for no reason. I didn't believe the place was haunted. I do now."

Just across the road, the old Newport Grammar School also has a ghost - thought to be that of the unfortunate King Charles I who stayed there in 1648. This story and a photograph of his phantom appear in *"More Ghosts of the Isle of Wight"*.

*The old town gibbet
once stood on this site
in Lower St James' Street*

Chapter Two

GHOSTS GALORE!

Some spirits have played a particularly lively part in Island history - spirits which warm the heart rather than chill the blood. If all our local smuggling yarns are to be believed, there's scarcely a cove or inlet of the Wight where tubs of contraband brandy have not come secretly ashore. What is certain is that during the great days of smuggling, from the mid-18th to the mid-19th century, Island smugglers and Island ghosts went hand in useful hand.

Tales of phantoms were told to keep honest folk abed. They wanted the lanes empty when they led their loaded ponies to churchyard or ruined cottage or side door of a great house. A ghost, they found worked wonders!

So where a spectre was said to have been seen ghastly in the moonlight, they made sure it was seen again, more often and looking even ghastlier. Roads running along the contraband coast "Back o' the Wight" had ghosts galore, Bonchurch, Chale and Brighstone went in for spectral stagecoaches, seen by few but heard by many. Although what was actually going bump in the night was kegs of brandy and fine wines. Brighstone, for good measure, boasted a flying phantom hare.

Ghostly riders whose steeds were whiter than white and silent as the grave, paraded along the Undercliff - much could be done with paint, a lantern in a hollowed turnip, and pads for a horse's hoofs. Many of these false spooks had a basis in folklore or fireside story; but where even the oldest and most credulous of caulkheads could not recall a midnight horror, then a horror was provided. Headless horsemen appeared as regularly as illegal liquor disappeared down Island throats.

All along the coasts, in the smugglers' finest hour, apparitions abounded. From his cave at Freshwater at appropriate intervals, crept the ghost of a French sailor said to have been cast ashore and to have starved to death in his hiding place. The lonely roads converging on the High Down Inn, Totland, once a smugglers' port of call, were haunted by two dead Preventive men who entered the inn.... but never left.

At Gurnard the local folk were kept in order by tales of the hanged boy they might see if they were foolish enough to stray abroad on certain nights - he had hanged himself with horse trappings in aptly-named

Harness Lane, and his roving spirit found no peace. In the sombre landscape swept by the salt winds of Newtown Creek, the menace was a madwoman whose ghost, eyes blazing and mouth stretched in a hideous grin, whipped a coach and four at frenzied speed in the lanes around London Heath. Sometimes she laughed aloud, and that was not good to hear!

From these fraudulent hauntings the simple villager, aware that he was up too late for his own good, fled in terror and spread his fears about him. Tales told in an inn corner on a windy winter night must have grown better with the telling. There would have been ale and encouragement a plenty. Perhaps only Preventive men noticed one curious coincidence: the ghosts always walked when the tides were right......

A DEAD HAND RAPPING....

Looking back, how artless and amusing it seems. Investigations however, have unearthed a modern haunting, a postscript to an old story whose ingredients are treachery, murder, a dead hand rapping at a bedroom door.

Part of the story is familiar. One West Wight smuggler, for either reward or revenge, informed on his comrades. They had a rich haul of smuggled brandy hidden at Clammerkin Bridge near Newtown. Now they planned to move it from the creek overland to a safe house. When? That very night, whispered the informer.

An ambush was laid. As the smugglers struggled with the heavy tubs in the dim light of covered lanterns, the Preventive men closed in. Their cry of "In the King's name!" was met by the flash of a flintlock pistol. The officers fired back. When the skirmish was over, two smugglers sprawled in their blood on the bridge while most of the others trudged sullenly towards Newtown, gaol and transportation.

Here the traditional story ends. What is not so well known is its sequel. Most of the desperate band were captured. Most, but unfortunately for the informer, not all. A handful broke out of the trap. They lay low, licked their wounds, and waited. Few secrets could be kept in their dangerous little world, except for those the Preventive men most wanted to know; and soon the survivors of what became known as the Battle of Clammerkin Bridge learned who had betrayed them. He was lured to an isolated cottage. The door was barred, the windows shuttered, and in semi-darkness on a summer's day he paid his debt in full. They were not content with a mere throat-slitting or a pistol to the head. They were in no hurry. When they had done their work, that cottage reeked like a slaughterhouse.

So much for the past. Yet that hideous past reaches out to the present with a ghostly hand, a hand that rapped on a bedroom door and night after night woke an Island farmer from his deepest sleep.

Ken Frogbrook once managed a farm in the West Wight, living in an old cottage on the estate. That cottage is the one in which the traitor was butchered. It was renovated, fitted with all the modern conveniences. Yet in it, a memory of murder long ago, lived on.

Ken is not the sort of man to be easily frightened but admits that when he first heard that menacing rat-tat-tat, he was alarmed. It was three o'clock in the morning. He was fast asleep after a tiring day, and so was his favourite working dog, curled up in its box in a corner of the bedroom. There was a knock on that bedroom door. Man and dog were suddenly awake. He threw on his clothes and flung open the door. There was no-one there.

He went back upstairs, where his dog was behaving oddly. Muzzle close to floorboards, hackles raised, it tracked to and fro on the landing, obviously puzzled. Ken was puzzled too. He was even more puzzled when that eerie rat-tat-tat came again on his bedroom door, and again there was nobody there. So it went on. He knew he was not dreaming. It happened night after night. "Eventually, I got used to it. I knew it would happen. I expected it."

Other people who spent time at the cottage proved less philosophical. There was a strange atmosphere, they said, something they could not describe but did not like. Ken's sister ran screaming out of the place after hearing the sound of someone walking in an empty bedroom. I will not identify the cottage here, in case current occupants are unaware of its history.

But every time Ken opened his bedroom door in answer to that urgent summons in the night he saw nothing. Knowing what happened in the house it may be better not to dwell upon what one night he might have seen.....

Chapter Three

SHADES OF SHANKLIN

GHOST IN GREASEPAINT

Ghosts seem to go with greasepaint. There have been many reports of haunted theatres, and most people will have heard of the famous Drury Lane ghost. But how many know that a ghost tried to get in on the act at an Island seaside show?

He was an old-time entertainer with the appropriately theatrical name of Albert DuBois. Albert recited monologues at the old Shanklin Pier Theatre in the 1890s but died after his second season. Though dead and buried he returned for an encore.

Show folk at Shanklin described the ghost as a greyish figure, tall, slightly bowed, with white hair. He was taken seriously by the local branch of Equity. Jokes of issuing him with a membership card apart, they once advised showgirls at the Pier Theatre not to remain there alone in case they became nervous. But there was nothing malign about Albert - the shade of a middle-aged man who must have given Victorian holidaymakers much moral sentiment in his monologue (incidentally he died at his mainland home, not on stage as stories say). But his presence could create an atmosphere that was unnerving to the nervous.

"You would be walking along backstage," said Jon Garr, organist and entertainer. "Suddenly, without any cause, you would step into an area of coldness. It usually happened when you were going down the steps from the stage to the dressing rooms.

"It was an uncanny experience, particularly at night. Sometimes when I was playing the organ I was certain someone was watching from the wings. Singers who appeared at the theatre said the same thing." Did they hear a ghostly echo of applause?

One telling piece of evidence supported the belief that was it Albert who lingered on. He appeared at the original Shankin Pier Theatre which, in 1918, was reduced to a heap of ashes after a disastrous fire. Another theatre was built on the same site. The old theatre had seven steps leading up to the stage. The second one had nine.

More than once, Jon Garr, alone in the place, heard footsteps as if someone was coming up on to the stage. He counted them. There were always seven....

Shanklin Pier Theatre has now gone - along with the pier. But what has become of its ghost, Albert DuBois?

Shanklin Pier Theatre is now gone, demolished along with the pier. Some fittings and fixtures were sold and in 1979 its plush red velvet seats went to a new home, Trinity Theatre at Cowes. But what of Albert? Has the curtain come down on this harmless theatrical ghost? Perhaps not, for members of the Cowes Operatic and Dramatic Society sometimes hear footsteps in the empty theatre. They move down the centre of auditorium, to and from the stage - which is impossible - because there's no central aisle. Albert has yet to make an appearance, but it would seem that he still likes to tread the boards.....

Albert's latest performance and the story of ghostly bloodstained footprints at Trinity Theatre appear in *More Ghosts of the Isle of Wight*.

THE CASE OF THE GREY LADY

Policemen in one part of the Island call their ghost the Grey Lady. She loiters with unknown intent in Shanklin police station. One constable has heard her twice. On duty at the station in the early hours of the morning he was startled by the sound of chairs being dragged across the floor in the canteen upstairs. The canteen was empty. Another PC also heard noises there when he knew the place was locked and vacant.

A constable and his family occupied a flat above the station. One day a heavy fire door opened wide. "You couldn't have closed that properly," the officer told his wife. Before she could reply, his son, then aged four, spoke up. "Oh no, Daddy," he said. "That's the lady." Despite questioning, he refused to say anything more about "the lady". All he would do, when the subject was raised, was smile. His father is positive that the boy had never heard stories about the station being haunted, and didn't seem at all upset.

It is fair to add that some police officers suspected the noises in the night were merely evidence of expansion and contraction of the building's metal frame. But elderly Shanklin residents will recall that in 1943, the town was devastated by German bombing in a single air raid. At 4.30pm on Sunday, 3rd January, four enemy aircraft flew in low from the sea, strafed the town with machine-gun fire, then dropped high explosive bombs.

No fewer than 23 people - thirteen men, nine women and a child were killed when a deadly cargo of high explosive bombs destroyed both the Roman Catholic Church in Atherley Road and Landguard Road Fire Station. The bomb which fell on the fire station, situated at the former Gloucester Hotel and Garage (now the town's Somerfield supermarket) killed one firewoman, nine firemen and two dispatch riders. A terrace of cottages a few yards away was virtually demolished by the blast. Shanklin Police Station was later built where they stood - on the corner of Landguard Road and Cross Street. Could the clue to the haunting at the police station lie amid the debris of that savage afternoon's work by the Luftwaffe? The case of the Grey Lady remains unsolved.

Chapter Four

WHY THE BLUE LADY WEPT

LOVE BEYOND THE GRAVE

A young girl's ghost was happy in death as well as life - until the living robbed her of what she loved most. She is a sweet ghost, a charming ghost, and her story has a happy ending. It's the story of a young girl and the pet dog she loved beyond the grave.

In the 19th century, smugglers exploited the Blue Lady of Nettlestone for their own purposes, sending her ever further afield to keep credulous folk in their beds while the boats came in. But there is a real Blue Lady whose 200-year-old history has a chapter which is very much up to date. This story came from a descendant of her family, the late Sheila White, who lived at The Duver, St. Helens.

The Priory at Nettlestone, standing on the site of a mediaeval priory, is a large house in a superb setting, parts of which date back to the 16th century. It was in Sheila's family from about 1700 to the 1920s, and as a child visiting the Island she fell in love with the old place. "It had everything that an old house ought to have, tales of secret rooms, secret passages, buried treasure, smugglers and of course, a ghost!"

Sheila was particularly impressed by the full-length portrait of a girl which hung in the dining room. "I adored it," she said. The young girl's gentle face and enigmatic smile still cast their spell. She wears a blue dress edged with silver lace, and there is silver lace at her cuffs. On her wrist perches a canary held by a satin ribbon; at her feet frisks a King Charles spaniel. This is the Blue Lady of Nettlestone Priory, who was so devoted to that dog that her shade wept for him from beyond the grave.

She appears to be about 14 years old, and died soon after her portrait was painted. It is her ghost who has been seen tripping down the main staircase or crossing the hall, playing with a ghostly dog in the grounds of the Priory or walking in nearby fields and on the road leading down to the sea. In her bedroom, a little panelled chamber containing a small four-poster bed, the faint scent of lavender would sometimes fill the air, and once, Sheila heard the faint swish of silken skirts, the sound of a tinkling laugh, and felt a sudden chill in the air.

Nettlestone Priory, where the Blue Lady walked in search of her dog.

Now apart from her portrait the Blue Lady was present only in spirit form. Her dog was present physically. He had been stuffed, and was hanging in a case over the stairs where, as a girl, Sheila used to look at him wide-eyed, almost expecting him to bark at her as the flame from her bedside candle wavered its reflection in the glass. She remembered being terrified by him. But he was very much a part of her childhood as was his long-dead mistress, and it was with sadness that she learned that the Priory was her family's house no more. In 1927 cousin Laura Spencer-Edwards who owned it died, and it was sold to an American woman.

IS THIS PLACE HAUNTED?

"In the very formal manner of the day Sheila's grandmother left her card. There came an invitation

to tea. One summer's day Sheila, her mother and grandmother strolled through the fields to meet the new resident at the Priory - and to hear an extraordinary story. As they were taking tea, the American woman suddenly asked, "Is this place haunted?"

"Yes," said Sheila. Her questioner silenced her. "Don't tell me a thing," she demanded. "Hear my story first." And then she told of the way her servants kept leaving. They could always be replaced, but when her butler

The Blue Lady and her little dog, happily reunited at last....

said he was going after 20 years' service she insisted on hearing his reasons. "Well, madam," he replied. "We can't stand the noises at night. We hear a child running along the corridors, sobbing and calling for her dog. It's heart-rending. We clearly hear the words 'my dog, my dog. What have you done with my dog'?" When staff left their rooms to find out what was happening they could see nothing - although the footsteps actually ran past them.

Convinced that her butler was telling the truth, his mistress investigated the tale. Local people knew of the ghostly girl but nothing of her dog - the apparition was always seen alone if it appeared beyond the Priory grounds. Then the head gardener remembered that a stuffed dog in a glass case had hung at the top of the stairs. Now it had gone, auctioned off with the former contents of the house. Seizing upon this clue, the new owner, with typical American vigour, started an Island-wide search. At last, as the result of an advertisement, she traced the stuffed dog to an antique shop in Newport, bought it for £1, and bore it back in triumph to the Priory.

This was her story. Now she asked, did they know what it was all about? Who was the ghost and was this her dog? And would that dreadful sobbing stop? She listened to what her guests had to tell her, then summoned a servant. Sheila pointed out the spot where the dog had hung. There and then the glass case went up in its old place over the stairs. And since that moment the Blue Lady of Nettlestone when she walks, walks quietly ...

Her portrait, alas, no longer hangs in the Priory dining room. She was seen gracing a country house near Guildford and was more recently inherited by a retired naval Commander living in Sussex. As for the little dog, he can still be seen at the Priory. There he stands above the stairs, secure in his glass case, a ginger and white Cavalier King Charles spaniel looking after two centuries, just a little weary.

The Priory is now the Priory Hotel, a family run establishment, and owner Ken Battle is taking no chances. He said the little dog would certainly not be moved while he was in charge....just in case.

But that's not the end of the story. For the glass case *was* moved and the little dog used to play a practical joke by a very foolish member of staff. Read about "The Dog's Revenge" in *More Ghosts of the Isle of Wight*.

THE GHOSTLY BAKER

Wisteria Cottage, the store and sub-post office which serves the village of Newchurch is blanketed by an enormous century-old wisteria vine, which in spring and early summer, is festooned with mauve blossoms. It has stood beside the village highway for more than 300 years. At one time in the 1800s pigs were slaughtered there. In later years, right up to the turn of the century, it was a bakery. Wisteria Cottage is haunted by a smell. Fortunately for owners, Joy and John Sandwell, if there's a ghost at work in the old building he's the baker not the slaughterman.

Although Wisteria Cottage now boasts tiny tea rooms, bread is baked there no longer. So when the exquisite and mouth-watering smell of fresh loaves fills the room, the Sandwells and their customers know the ghostly baker is busy again. Previous owners Barbara and Neville St John Jacobs noticed the appetising aroma many times in the years they were there. Sometimes the long-dead baker was busy making meat pies and puddings, at other times it was crusty bread.

After they took over Wisteria Cottage in 1986, the Sandwells noticed the phantom baker at work on just a few occasions. "It is very localised, a strong, old-fashioned smell of baking bread - which you just

Every Shrove Tuesday local children gathered at Wisteria Cottage to sing for their pennies and sweets.

don't get nowadays," Joy said. "It lasts for about half a minute and then vanishes, as if it has been switched off."

Once and only once has the cottage been filled with what previous owner, Barbara Jacobs, described as "a vile smell," the pungent odour of burning hides and carcasses. Both she and her shop assistant wrinkled their noses at it and were discussing what could have sent it sweeping through the store when, "as if cut with a knife" it vanished.

Customers familiar with the haunting odour joke, "He's baking again" when they smell his efforts. It is accepted nowadays as just something that happens and familiarity has bred content. Today though, the village shop is more likely to be filled with the pungent aroma of garlic which is grown and picked locally. Many farm workers and packers from nearby Langbridge Farm use the stores and bring in the smell on their clothing and shoes. "Sometimes the whole building reeks of garlic. There is no way the baker can compete with that and I am beginning to wonder whether the garlic might have driven him away," laughed Joy.

The little bakery was for many years at the hub of village life. It was here, in front of the Post Office every Shrove Tuesday, that local children would sing the traditional Shroving Song. At midday, they would pack away slates and books and follow their teachers around the village in traditional fashion to sing for goodies. The baker, in flour dusted cap and apron, would fling a shower of cakes and pennies into their midst, then the children would hurry off to the vicarage and nearby Veniscombe House to sing for more pennies and sweets.

GHOST-GIRL AT TUMBLEWEED

Does one of these children haunt the place where in life she would have scrapped for shroving treasures with her classmates a century ago? When Jean and Peter Cooper drove through the village early one Sunday morning they noticed her standing at the side of the road. However, the child wearing an old-fashioned long dress and a poke bonnet did not seem aware of them at all.

It was August 1985, and the Coopers, who now live in Palmers Road, Wootton, were enjoying their annual fortnight's holiday on the Island. Keen treasure hunters, they were on their way from Wroxall to Ryde to use their metal detector on the beach. "It was 6.30am, everyone in the village was still in bed, there was not a soul about and no other traffic on the roads," Jean recalled.

As the couple rounded the bend just before Veniscombe and Newchurch Post Office, they noticed a child aged about eight, standing at the side of the road outside Tumbleweed Cottage. "It was as if she was dressed up for a fancy dress party or a Victorian Day at the nearby primary school. She was standing there looking towards the church, but as our car reached her she didn't turn or glance towards it, she didn't seem to be aware of us at all," said Jean.

Peter, an ex-serviceman and retired bank manager, remembers that the strange child wore a blue dress which came to just above her ankles, white socks or stockings and shoes. The most striking thing was her light-blue peaked bonnet. "We drove past her and it was not until we had gone down Newchurch Shute that we looked at one another and asked ourselves why such a young girl had been out so early in the morning in that old-fashioned costume. There was something off-key and unnatural about what we saw," said Jean.

Peter added, "It was quite weird. She looked real but it was somehow all wrong. She was out of time and out of place. Perhaps we should have turned back to see if she was there still. I suspect she would have vanished."

ANNABELLE OF ARRETON MANOR

A brutal family murder lies behind the most persistent of Arreton Manor's many hauntings. The story goes that when Barnaby Leigh, member of a family of wealthy Island landowners, and tenants of the manor in Elizabethan times, lay sick in his bed, his son John, over-eager for his inheritance smothered him with a pillow. John's small sister, Annabelle, saw him do it. Her brother dragged her screaming into an upstairs room - where an area of coldness can be felt today, even in the warmest weather - and pushed her through a window to her death.

Annabelle returns regularly. In spite of her gruesome death she doesn't seem too unhappy, although her little cry of "Mamma, mamma" has a pathetic air. She has been seen by staff and visitors as she walks through the manor house and its gardens. Ivy Welstead of Lake, who worked for many years as receptionist at the manor, heard her before she saw her. In the middle of the evening came footsteps, followed by that cry. One of the children of the house she thought, but all the children there were in bed asleep. Then, one autumn night, there was poor little Annabelle standing at the top of the main staircase. Ivy saw her clearly in full electric light. The little figure wore a blue dress reaching almost

Haunted Arreton Manor.

down to white slippers laced criss-cross with ribbon, and her fair hair fell in tight curls. She remained there for a moment and then faded away.

In the gardens, too, Ivy heard that childish voice from long ago and caught a glimpse of Annabelle. Among visitors who have seen her was a girl of about the same age who came running back to

Ivy Welstead talking to the spirits of Arreton Manor. Photo by Brian Aldrich.

her mother crying, "I've just seen a little girl in a blue dress - and she walked right through the wall."

As befits such an historic manor house, Arreton abounds in ghosts. There is a figure in silvery-grey associated with the fragrance of spring flowers - an almost overpowering sweetness encountered by visitors in various parts of the building. The ghostly smell of incense is thought to originate from the time that Arreton was owned by the Abbey of Quarr. Perhaps the grave chanting of monks is also an echo from those four centuries long ago. Also accompanied by the scents of spring, is the ghost of a woman in a tight-waisted, puff-sleeved dress of deep cherry red - a woman with long, curly black hair, whose face is never seen.

Apart from such sounds as footsteps, the rustle of a skirt and Annabelle's voice, the late Leslie Slade (also known as Count Slade de Pomeroy) who owned and lived at the manor with his wife and family, was often woken by mysterious rappings on his bedroom door. No-one was ever there. Ivy who is a medium herself, took these manorial hauntings as part of her day's work. Count Slade was talking to her one day in an otherwise empty room when he felt a push in the back. "Don't take any notice," advised Ivy. "Two monks just came through and one of them bumped against you."

When the Slades finally left after 25 years, the next owners, Nick and Jeanne Schroeder, reported that the manor's ghosts seemed perturbed by the changes and staff had complained that spectral monks haunting the tea rooms were particularly bothersome. "When we first moved here in 1984 I found the place quite unnerving and eerie, especially at night. But that feeling quickly dissipated and I have never met any of the ghosts," admitted Jeanne.

They are however, still around. The overpowering smell of pungent old-fashioned tobacco smoke appears from nowhere, a lame ghost with a stick or crutch is heard tap-tapping his way upstairs, and friends of the family staying in the west bedroom with its carved four-poster bed, were startled one night to see a dark haired woman in a white shift glide across the room and vanish straight through the window....

Chapter Five

MURDER, MADNESS AND MALICE AT KNIGHTON GORGES

From the high downs the road drops to a valley. Driving, you come without warning upon two decaying stone pillars, all that is left of a magnificent gateway. Sheep graze as rabbits scuttle among a wilderness of brambles and cow-parsley. You can see a stone barn, a waterworks, a wood, the ivy-shrouded remnant of a broken wall. That is all. But walk carefully. You are walking on haunted ground.

The mystery of Knighton Gorges in the parish of Newchurch casts an enduring spell. The Elizabethan manor house which once dominated the valley - an old picture shows it massively gabled and high-chimneyed - has been gone for almost two centuries; but here time passes slowly, and the past throws its shadow on the present in a story which includes a sudden death, insanity, a malicious life and a gallery of ghosts.

Knighton Manor has had a colourful history, and the colour includes blood-red. Hugh de Morville, one of its earliest feudal owners, assisted in the murder of Thomas a Becket in Canterbury Cathedral. He and his ruthless friends then took ship for shelter at Carisbrooke Castle and when the hue and cry died down, he retired to his estate at Knighton until his death 30 years later.

From the de Morvilles it passed to Sir Ralph de Gorges, a Crusader who sought and found holy death fighting the infidel. The manor was later held by other families and played its part in Island history; but it was from the coming of the Dillingtons of Dorset and the building of the great Elizabethan house that its ghostly heritage springs.

THE ROOM OF TEARS

From a gloomy oak-panelled chamber known as the "Room of Tears" the first whispers of the supernatural stirred. Fascinated by these tales, Anthony Dillington took care to preserve much of the old building when the house was remodelled in 1560. Intrigued by the Room of Tears, he even had the name carved over the door. But as years passed, ghostly music and sounds of sobbing gave way to groans and rattling chains. Thuds and scrapes were heard and objects were hurled about the room. A priest from Brading performed an exorcism and the incident was celebrated in a contemporary poem.

> "Then with book and bell and chaunt and pray'r,
> Up and down the haunted stair
> He drove the Unseen to and fro."

Skipping a fascinating century, we find Knighton Gorges held by Sir Tristram Dillington, MP for Newport, Major in the Guards, breeder of fine horses. One story handed down by Newchurch folk has him married with four children to carry on the Dillington line. Then tragedy struck. In 1721, according to legend, his entire family contracted a fever. Within a fortnight his wife and children were dead. Sir Tristram, frantic with grief, killed himself.

The probable truth is less romantic. Sir Tristram, at 43, had no wife or children. A bachelor with two spinster sisters Mary and Hannah, he lived a lonely life at Knighton Gorges. He was apparently a reckless gambler and subject to fits of depression. Whether he drowned himself in the pond shown in that old print, or shot himself, is unclear.

The once great house at Knighton Gorges was demolished in 1821.
From an engraving by Englefield.

Whichever method he chose, as a suicide, his property should have gone to the Crown. But on discovering his body, his good and faithful steward turned his master's favourite horse, Thunderbolt, loose with a broken girth and spread the story of a riding accident. The estate was saved. The grateful sisters rewarded him with a farm.

However he met his end, Sir Tristram has slept fitfully since. It was not long after his death on July 7, that local folk began to avoid Knighton Shute after dark. A spectral hound was seen, followed by a headless horseman. From a sealed room in the old house came an agony of wailing. Through the succeeding centuries there have been numerous reports of Sir Tristram's ghost driving a coach and four on the anniversary of his death - half a dozen of them in the past 50 years.

SCANDAL AND MADNESS

In the mid-18th century, by which time the manor had descended through the female line to General Maurice Bocland, Knighton Gorges entertained distinguished guests. David Garrick met John Wilkes, once a member of the notorious Hellfire Club, there. Sir Joshua Reynolds stayed. Wit flowed with the wine, and the marriage of the general's eldest daughter into an ancient Scottish family seemed to herald fresh glories for the Island house. In fact that marriage was its doom. Maurice George Bisset was born.

It was this Captain Bisset who made the Island and two of its mansions, Knighton Gorges and Appuldurcombe, familiar names in every London coffee house. He ran off with Seymour, the beautiful wife of Sir Richard Worsley of Appuldurcombe, an officer of the Royal Household, and Sir Richard sued him for £20,000. The case was a sensation. Copies of the evidence were hawked in the London streets, and Captain Bisset suffered from one of Gillray's most savage caricatures.

Neither party came out of it well. Lady Worsley admitted to having 27 lovers - and venereal disease - while Sir Richard was said to have condoned his wife's promiscuity. The jury agreed with Sir Richard. His wife's affections had indeed been alienated. But they only awarded him one shilling damages.

Humiliated and bitter, Maurice George Bisset returned to the Island. Shunned by society, he was no longer welcome in fashionable circles. An exception to this was Lady Harriet Mordaunt who married Bisset after a brief courtship. They lived quietly at Knighton Gorges, producing two daughters, Jane Harriet and Anne.

But Seymour had left him with a parting gift. Syphilis slowly poisoned both body and mind, and when his eldest daughter, Jane, announced her engagement to her cousin the Reverend Fenwick, Bisset forbade the marriage. The pair ignored him. Bisset swore that she and her husband would never set foot in the house. They thought little of the threat since it was part of the bride's entail. But Maurice George Bisset kept his word. He enlisted an army of workmen and ordered them to demolish what had been described as "by far the most considerable and beautiful of the ancient mansions of the Island." Down tumbled the tall red-brick chimneys, down crashed the roof of ancient moss-covered tiles, the gables, the mullioned windows. As the year ended, so did the life of a noble house. When its last owner died too, at his Scottish estate, Lessendrum, on December 16, 1821, only the cellars and the gateposts were left. The fine grey stone, roof tiles, carved staircases and other materials salvaged from the house were incorporated in other Island homes, where some can still be seen today.

But has the ancient manor of Knighton Gorges gone for ever? Or does it still exist beyond the bounds of space and time? A foolish question to ask, one thinks, standing on a grassy mound where the past is covered by pine trees. And yet.....

A STRANGE STORY

Some elderly Islanders have a strange story to tell. It's about a young man who knocked on a Newchurch door one winter night and asked for lodgings. During supper he told the family how annoyed he'd been a little earlier that evening. He was peering up a drive which led to a big house when a carriage and horses came thundering down. He scarcely had time to leap aside, and strode somewhat shakily up to the house to complain.

There was the sound of music and laughter but no-one replied to his knock on the door. One window threw a shaft of light into the darkness and through a crack in the curtains he saw a crowded drawing room. Evidently a fancy dress party was in full swing, with everyone in Georgian costume. He had rapped on the window but was ignored, so had walked on to Newchurch. Where was the house? He took out his map and tried to show them. There was no house, but he was pointing to the site of Knighton Gorges.

Then consider the statements of Miss Ethel C. Hargrove, Island author of a number of travel books. There are many reports of supernatural music being heard in the neighbourhood of Knighton Gorges usually on a New Year's Eve. With a friend, she visited the site of the old house on New Year's Eve, 1915. There it stood, restored. They saw its lights, they heard the baying of dogs and the sound of carriages jingling to its door. They watched a man in 18th century dress raise his glass in a toast.

She wrote, "A few minutes before midnight a flood of melody arose from the site of the former mansion. It was varied in character - dance music played on a harpsichord. Georgian minuet airs, slow and stately, then a duet between tenor and soprano voices. At twelve the party seemed to break up, a pistol or gun was fired, dogs bayed, and the sound of carriage wheels was heard."

PUZZLE OF THE PILLARS

In 1972 Knighton Gorges made news again, when the late Ted Perry of Brading wrote to the IW County Press to ask what had happened to the figures which adorned the old gateposts until, as he put it, "a few weeks ago." His letter was followed by another from a Shanklin woman recalling that the pillars had been surmounted by animals looking like a cross between a lion and a dog. Yet photographs dating back to 1916 showed nothing but the large stone roundels known locally as "the loaves of bread."

As a coach driver, Ted frequently passed the gateposts and pointed them out to visitors! He would have been willing to bet that the animal figures were there - and three friends he took to see the gateposts said they had noticed them too. Over the years many others have seen what evidently isn't there and recent photographs of these gateposts have also revealed poltergeist lights. These can be seen in Isle of Wight Ghosts Book Four while other haunting tales of Knighton Gorges are contained in More Ghosts of the Isle of Wight.

Knighton Gorges is now recognised as the Island's most haunted place. It exerts a strange fascination for many and scores of ghost-

The old stone gateposts to the long vanished house of Knighton Gorges. Ghostly stone creatures and poltergeist lights have been seen on top of these pillars.

hunters gather there every New Year's Eve hoping to see the house reappear. The manor house was demolished almost two centuries ago, but something lives on there, where a ruined gateway leads to a haunted hill.

Chapter Six

HAUNTING TALES OF WINES AND SPIRITS

The haunted inn is perhaps more easily found in fiction that in fact. It stands, of course, at a crossroads. It has a ruinous air and a shifty landlord. Its weather-beaten sign creaks under a fitful moon - many a lonely traveller rues the night he spent at "The Hanged Man". The Isle of Wight has its fair share of haunted hostelries, including one which inexplicably disappeared never to be seen again. Read about this unwelcoming ghost pub and its strange regulars in *More Ghosts of the Isle of Wight*.

THE HOLE IN THE WALL

The Hole in the Wall at Ventnor hasn't yet vanished, but after "Time" was called there some years ago, it never re-opened. The Hole was named originally after the door leading from the Central Hotel to an ostlers' room through which beer was passed after hours. Many tankards must have passed this way, for Pound Lane was full of farriers and up to 300 horses were stabled nearby.

In 1860 a beer licence was granted to the Hole, which officially became the Commercial Tap. Locals still referred to these old coachmen's quarters and coal store as the Hole in the Wall. With this colourful history it's not surprising that the little alehouse had two ghosts. One of them, popped into the lounge bar occasionally, and former landlord Dick Ring saw it twice.

"I would be at the bar drawing a beer, then I would suddenly get a feeling that a customer had come in. I would look up just in time to catch sight of a figure, a tall man in an old-fashioned, light-coloured suit moving through the bar. He went right to the far corner and disappeared."

June Ring encountered the other ghost at the Hole in the Wall. She woke up one night to find a figure in uniform with a high military collar standing over her bed. She sat up, put out a frightened hand, and the phantom faded away. Imagination? Perhaps her two sons, then aged nine and 11, imagined something too. Minutes later they came running in, obviously alarmed, shouting that there was a strange man in their bedroom. There was, of course, no-one.

SOMETHING IN THE CELLARS

Equally puzzling are the activities of whatever has made its home in the cellars of the Partlands Hotel, Ryde. It's a little menacing and certainly mischievous. The pub has changed hands a number of times in recent years, but most licensees have a tale or two to tell about its unquiet spirits.

For one thing, most dogs don't like the cellars. One landlord had two collies who would never go down the steps. And an old boxer belonging to Olive and Tom Bowden, former licensees, went down once - just once. His ears pricked, his hair stood on end and he dashed back upstairs. They found him sitting in the kitchen, shivering with terror.

But Betty Buckett, a landlady there in the 1960s, recalled something odder than an eerie feeling among the beer barrels. "One night when there were only about half a dozen people in the bar, my husband was playing darts. One chap was marking and the others were chatting to me. My husband raised his arm to throw a dart, but instead turned round, looking annoyed. "Who pushed me?" he demanded. No-one was anywhere near him. "Somebody poked my arm," he said. "We couldn't understand it." Nor could she understand whose voice it was that whispered her name - her son heard it too - when her husband hadn't spoken and there was no-one else about.

Olive Bowden was sure there was something odd about parts of the Partlands Hotel. When she was ill and found it difficult to get upstairs, she decided to sleep on the ground floor. "I would always wake up at the same time, about three in the morning. There would be a strange smell in the room, a musty, earthy smell, and a kind of coldness. I felt as if something had come in, something uncanny. It's hard to convey what it was like. Anyway, I moved back to my bedroom. I never slept downstairs again." She had been sleeping directly above the cellars.

Tom Bowden took a sceptical view. "I don't believe this claptrap about ghosts," he said firmly, but then added, "I could never understand how the taps on the gas cylinders were turned off." In the cellars are the gas cylinders which force beer up to the bar. They are the type commonly used in pubs. Each has its own tap and these taps are not easy to turn. A spanner is used on them. Despite tales of a secret tunnel there is only one entrance to the cellars. No-one could go down without his knowledge, yet on some busy nights the beer pressure suddenly failed, he went down to see what was wrong - and found the taps turned off. It happened many times.

"A real nuisance," he admitted. And, though still firmly disbelieving in ghosts, he also admitted that if he put down a tool or a paintbrush while working in the cellars it was unlikely to be there when he turned to pick it up again. Somehow or other it would be moved yards away.

Was Lily Deacon murdered here?

Could the murder of a Victorian barmaid have anything to do with the curious happenings at this Ryde pub? Locally it's said so and this story is explored further in *Ghosts of the Isle of Wight III*. At one time what is thought to be her name - Lily Deacon - was scrawled all over the cellar ceiling in black capital letters. Past licensees, saw it. By the name was the date 1896. An elderly customer recalled a story about Lily the barmaid, meeting death at the hands of her jealous husband or lover, down there where some dogs won't go. That old lath and plaster ceiling has disappeared now and the name of Lily Deacon with it. The mystery remains. How do those gas taps get turned off?

BUXOM BETTY AND THE BLACKSMITH'S ARMS

Buxom Betty the smuggler's daughter who met a bad end two centuries ago is said to haunt the area around the Blacksmith's Arms, not far from Carisbrooke on the main Newport-Calbourne Road. The arms in which Betty frequently found herself were not those of the blacksmith but of the various excise men associated with the 18th century Admiralty Cottages not far from the inn. By a happy coincidence she was at her most amorous and available when contraband was due to pass through this junction on a busy smuggling route. The excise men, one presumes, failed to keep their minds on their work.

Alas for Betty, so did she. She fell in love with one of the officers she entertained and betrayed her smuggler friends. Some were captured. Some escaped, and these came back for Betty. They strangled her. A scream that sinks to something worse than a scream may still echo in nearby Betty Haunt Lane

So much for the story. The derivation of Betty Haunt may mean "bad haunt" or perhaps "Betty's aunt" even "Betty's pound" as a horse and cattle pound is said to have existed in the lane at one time. Nevertheless, the Blacksmith's Arms and the fields and tracks round it keep their haunted reputation. Two murders in this century, the last in the early 1960s when a former landlady was killed, have helped - though in the present pub's homely atmosphere it's hard to believe they happened. But there have been some disturbing incidents at the 400-year-old building, once a hunting lodge and later a staging post for smugglers.

When Wilfred Cuming took over the pub after the landlady's violent death, his dog howled for three nights running. Each night it began to howl at precisely 3am. When Peter Drewery and his wife took on the pub, their dog howled and refused to follow them along a passage near the front bar. At night mysterious sounds, raps and knockings were heard. Once, at about 12.30am, the couple were in the kitchen when they were startled by a loud thump on the kitchen door. For a moment they thought someone must

Murder was committed here at the lonely Blacksmith's Arms.

have broken in. But when Peter went to investigate he found no intruder and the pub was still locked and secure. Pat Drewery said, "I didn't like staying there overnight by myself. Believe me, if Peter was away I kept the lights on ..."

When Donna and Edgar Nieghorn took over the pub in 1994, they were sceptical of its haunted reputation. However the new licensees always experienced great difficulty finding anyone to look after the Blacksmith's Arms when they wanted time off. Two young men who did agree won't be doing it again. "When we came home they were in quite a state," said Donna. "All the cupboards in their attic room had opened by themselves - not once but several times."

And at 11.30pm one dark and stormy night in October 1996, a group of friends left the pub. One of them was a 42-year-old Newport woman whom I will call Sue, as she prefers to remain anonymous. She is not a believer in ghosts or the supernatural, but that night she caught a brief glimpse of the inn's dark past. As she made her way to the car park, Sue noticed a man wearing a cloak and hood, standing by the wall. He was not very tall, and his head was bowed, his face hidden. For just a few seconds he stood there, then as Sue watched, he just faded into nothingness. No-one else had noticed him. As she hurried to her car, the shivers she felt were nothing to do with the chill of the night.

WHAT WALKS IN BETTY HAUNT LANE?

Nearby in Betty Haunt Lane, a brush with the supernatural almost proved fatal for an elderly Lancashire woman holidaying on the Island with her husband and friends. Shortly after a terrifying encounter with a ghost, she suffered a serious heart attack and spent the remainder of her holiday in the Coronary Care Unit at St Mary's Hospital, Newport.

Describing her unnerving experience to nursing staff there, Mary Breedon became quite agitated. "We had been for a drink or two at the Blacksmith's Arms pub and we were walking back down the long narrow lane. It was almost dark and my friend and I linked arms with my husband. I heard the sound of running footsteps behind us and turned to see who it was. There was no-one there, but I could clearly hear a woman's ragged and rapid breathing. It sounded as if she was terrified and she was running for her life".

The unseen woman rushed straight *through* then past Mary, and as she fled on down the darkening lane, Mary caught a brief glimpse of her - enough to see that she was dressed in an old-fashioned long skirt and shawl, with hair tumbling about her shoulders as she ran. Mary stopped dead in the middle of the road, unable to believe what she had just seen. She felt an icy coldness where the ghost had passed through her.

Incredibly, neither her husband Bill, nor her friend had seen or heard anything. "What's the matter love?" asked Bill. "You have gone absolutely white. You look just like you have seen a ghost."

BELL, BOOK AND CANDLE.....

Other Island inns have had their stories in the past - at the former Bugle Hotel in Newport an impertinent spirit is said to have plucked plugs from the sinks and sent them floating up on to draining boards, while its cousin at the George Hotel in Yarmouth, apparently had the habit of dabbling in cosmetics left on a dressing table.

Clatterford House, Carisbrooke, once home of the well-known Brannon printing family who founded the IW County Press, has long been said to be haunted by the ghost of a family member. This Edwardian ghost, dressed most respectably and wearing her lace cap, would appear in a corridor. Later owners, in a manner by which she would surely not have been amused, referred to her as "Clattie." Although a gentle ghost, it's said that she was once exorcised with bell, book and candle or whatever rites were thought appropriate by the local parson. It seems the parson omitted some necessary ceremonial for the ghost has shown no inclination to move on..... yet.

In recent times Clatterford House has been run as an hotel, restaurant and also as a pub known as The Shute Inn. In October 1996 the old house, dating back to Elizabethan times, changed hands again. Owner John Adams announced plans to turn the clock back more than two centuries, returning Clatterford House to its 18th century glory as a private family home. However the restaurant, re-named the Brannon Restaurant, remains - as does the ghost.

A photograph of her hangs on the restaurant wall. Her name was Elizabeth Brannon and according to a hand-written note on the back of her likeness, she died from a broken neck in 1908, in a curious accident after falling down three steps into a bedroom. Local folk however had their own theories. Her death was no accident. She took her own life after an unhappy love affair, it was whispered.

The mysterious circumstances surrounding her death may account for her spirit lingering at Clatterford House. The passage of time evidently means little to this gentle ghost. She continues to glide

Clatterford House, home to a gentle ghost.

along that corridor and disappear down those three steps. She is still seen - despite the parson's best efforts - and her harmless wanderings bother nobody. June Mills who worked as a cook has seen her in the kitchens and felt a presence in that corridor.

"I am not a believer in ghosts but I have been forced to believe in this one," said John Adams. In common with hauntings elsewhere, lights at Clatterford House are often switched off - and another telling sign - objects are moved from room to room by unseen hands. John is remarkably philosophical about the presence. "She is quite harmless. You could not have a nicer ghost. It is her home too and I am quite proud to have her here."

A MISTY SHAPE

A stone's throw from Clatterford is the tiny hamlet of Plaish, near Bowcombe. Here at Plaish Farmhouse, an elderly ghost has been seen countless times by the Chick family who have farmed there for generations.

It was after a death in the family that one encounter came. Alone in the house, Mrs Chick walked out of an upstairs room to go down and open the front door. To her surprise she saw an elderly man with a long white beard on the landing. Bewildered, she found herself standing aside to let the old gentleman pass - but then his figure blurred into a misty shape and he floated down the stairs. Cameron Chick who has seen the apparition at close quarters inside the house and twice from the

Plaish Farmhouse, near Carisbrooke.

outside when it stood at an upstairs window, confirms her description. It is white and looks as if it is composed of smoke or water-vapour.

In spite of its ethereal nature, the Plaish ghost makes itself heard. This usually happens after dark. The family believe that its home is in a large cupboard in a certain bedroom - and that bedroom is always cold. It walks from that bedroom along a passage and down the stairs. The tread is deliberate and unmistakable although the passage is carpeted, so footsteps there cannot normally be heard.

Cameron Chick used to sleep in that bedroom until he married. Like the rest of the family he accepts the ghost is harmless, although he had one bad experience there. He woke to discover something undefinable pressing down on his face. For a moment he couldn't breathe. Then, as he struggled for air it disappeared. He refused to sleep in the room again.

The family can provide no history for their ghost. He inhabits the oldest part of the house, which dates back to the 17th century. Is there any connection with a labourer who apparently drowned in the farm sheepwash many years ago? They don't know. But now and again, when night falls, something is there.

This story was originally written in 1977. Plaish Farmhouse remains in the Chick family - Cameron, Penny, and their four children live there now. As well as helping with the farm, Penny runs holiday cottages and takes bed and breakfast visitors in the farmhouse.

They had the farmhouse blessed by a local clergyman when they first moved in, and despite structural alterations the ghost remained silent. But in April 1996, he started to walk again.

"We hear him all over the house now and he has been seen several times. Cameron glimpsed him standing at a bedroom window and he has been seen on the stairs. Perhaps the ages of the children have something to do with it. The house is always full of youngsters and teenagers, perhaps their energy attracts him," said Penny.

One night in January 1997, something unseen climbed into bed with family friend Jonathan Farmer when he stayed in the farmhouse. "It was about 2.30am when I felt something sitting on the bed beside me. The mattress actually went down as if there was a weight there. But there was no-one in the bed but me.

"I put out a tentative foot and felt an incredible, intense icy chill emanating from whatever was sharing the old brass bed with me. I edged away from it pretty quickly. It was like having someone with very cold feet in bed with you!" said Jonathan.

Perhaps the ghost likes to take an occasional nap, for Penny has noticed the clear indentations of a body appearing on beds after she has made them. And the ghost is also a touch light-fingered. Books are a favourite target. The childrens' exercise books and Cameron's farm stock book have caught his fancy and vanished - but always turn up again after a few days.

Penny and Cameron believe the Plaish ghost to be a protective spirit who likes to keep an eye on the family. "This is actually a very warm and friendly house. Having him around doesn't bother us at all - guests who stay here are fascinated to hear that the house is haunted." Penny added, "If he really wants to be helpful perhaps he can be persuaded to tell us the winning lottery numbers - as he must owe us a few years' rent!"

THE GOOD-LUCK GHOST

The Chicks may have to share any lottery win with the fortunate folk at Comforts Farm, Northwood, where the Annett family have a ghost that brings them good luck. Their "guardian angel" they call her. The farmhouse in Pallance Road, an old building thought to stand on the site of a Roman camp, is haunted by a middle-aged woman who wears a pleated bodice, silk skirt, and white bonnet, flat at the top and back. And this phantom is one with a difference - she's seen only by men..

The late Albert Annett first saw her in 1968. He woke up suddenly to find her sitting in a chair in the bedroom. "She looked so real that I got up to touch her," he said, "but she just smiled at me and disappeared." The Annetts' grandson and son-in-law have seen the mysterious figure and so have guests - if they are male.

The "guardian angel" is completely accepted by the family. She has been seen in different rooms at different times of the year. But whenever she appears, some little stroke of good fortune always follows. But for men only!

In recent years however, she has made herself scarce - due perhaps to redecoration work at the farmhouse - the family think. "We rather miss her," said Glenn Annett rather wistfully. As a lad he saw the ghost several times as she glided about the house in her distinctive flat-topped bonnet. "We don't think she's left us for good because mysterious rappings and noises are sometimes heard. And now we have got the National Lottery, we could do with a bit of her good luck," said Glenn. "Perhaps we should try counting those raps - she might be trying to tell us something......"

THE PHANTOM BUTLER

Another phantom who still wants to be of service from beyond the grave can be found shuffling along the central passage at Norris Castle, East Cowes. His creaky, arthritic footsteps have been heard when the household are at dinner, and on one notable occasion an admiral and his lady were among dinner party guests who ran out to see who was making the sounds. All they saw was an empty passageway. Now he's allowed to buttle in peace. Everyone's used to him and even the dogs show no alarm. Occasionally he apparently attempts, in a properly respectful way, to draw attention to himself. He gives a cough. A small, deferential cough...

A ROYAL GHOST-DOG

Meanwhile at nearby Barton Manor, the shade of a small collie dog haunts the grounds. The manor itself has enjoyed a long and varied history as a farmhouse, a religious Augustinian Oratory and manor house. But it was with the coming of Victoria and Albert to the adjoining Osborne estate that Barton rose to prominence. The Queen bought Barton Manor in 1845 for £18,000 to use as an annexe to Osborne for visitors, and Prince Albert was let loose on the design and renovation work.

In his enthusiasm to modernise the Jacobean manor, he demolished ancient walls, gutted the interior, ripping out panelling and

Barton Manor, East Cowes, where a Royal ghost-dog plays.

fireplaces, and obliterated almost all traces of the Oratory. Albert also planned the gardens, complete with a skating lake for the Queen. However, Victoria did not allow mixed skating on this lake in the winter - as she feared ladies could be embarrassed if they fell while members of the opposite sex were present.

This skating lake is now a sunken water garden, while Barton Manor's vineyard and winery is a tourist attraction. The house, which is not open to the public, is the home of multi-millionaire film producer and music tycoon Robert Stigwood. According to staff, he has not seen the ghost....yet.

It was during the 1940s that Miss Holt lived there for a time with her family. A great collector of antiquarian IW books, she ran her own little bookshop in Nodehill, Newport. Despite the passage of more than half a century, Miss Holt could still describe her encounter with the little ghost-dog quite vividly. "I went out into the garden one morning and over by the big pond I noticed a dog. It was a small collie and I had no reason to think it was a ghost....until it faded away, vanishing before my eyes."

She later discovered that a little dog, said to have been one of the Queen's favourites, was drowned in that skating lake.

Chapter Seven

HAUNTINGS AT BILLINGHAM MANOR

Happily still standing, as it has stood for centuries, is Billingham that most elegant and haunted of manors where ghostly memories steal out of the past to the sound of sweet music and the scent of lilies.

Many tales have been told about Billingham. Eminent people have related their strange experiences there. Ghosts who have walked its panelled rooms, along its corridors, up its magnificent Inigo Jones staircase, include a woman in grey, a man in red and an invisible being with a beautiful voice. The severed head of Charles I is said to have shone with a phosphorescent glow from a secret recess. Dead men have fought duels in the moonlight. And poltergeist activity has been reported there on such a scale that the solid old building itself seemed to shake.

Yet there is nothing sinister in the atmosphere of Billingham. Former owners Elizabeth and Spencer Forbes who moved there in 1955 insisted, "It's not a creepy place at all." (In fact it is the Billingham story which started me writing the Isle of Wight Ghost Books. As a local journalist living nearby, I heard the manor was supposedly haunted and called round to see Elizabeth and Spencer to find out more. When my story appeared in the Isle of Wight County Press it prompted several letters from people who had other ghost stories to tell......In 1977 the original *Ghosts of the Isle of Wight* was born).

Approached by an avenue of trees, Billingham Manor lies in a secluded setting near Chillerton. To all appearances the house is a Georgian structure, but on closer inspection the Jacobean basement is revealed. Today its warm facade of red Georgian brick is welcoming, its interior gracious. As one of Britain's busiest haunts it has a quite unghostly charm. The rebuilding of the earlier stone structure took place when it was made over to Edward Worsley by the Worsleys of Appuldurcombe on his marriage to one of the Leigh girls from Northcourt, Shorwell. It stayed in the Worsley family until 1842 and became part of Shorwell Parish. Out of this marriage came the first of the manor's ghost stories. Edward's bride is said to have taken a lover, a Frenchman whom her husband challenged to a duel. Although he lost, the Frenchman sleeps soundly in his grave. It is the guilty ghost of the erring wife which walks the house and gardens; while the clash of swords has echoed through the centuries.

THE ETERNAL DUEL

Elizabeth Forbes heard the sound of that eternal duel. Among those reported to have seen the ghostly lady are an un-named publisher who visited Billingham during its sixteen-year occupation by J.B. Priestley in the 1930s and 1940s; Mr John Perks, who had the manor in the early 1950s; and Mr Perks' niece.

The publisher went there with playwright Jan de Hartog, and several times saw a smiling woman whom he took to be the housekeeper. She seemed so real that he didn't mention her until they were leaving. Then he learned that there was no housekeeper, and that with the Priestleys away, only the two of them were in the house. In June 1950, Mr Perks saw a hooded woman in a grey cloak passing him only a few feet away. Seconds later she had vanished. The same figure disappeared from the morning room a few weeks later after being followed there by his astonished niece.

Incidentally, Mr Priestley, who wrote a great number of his plays and novels at Billingham, was often said to know a great deal about its ghosts. As a believer that our consciousness survives bodily death, he would not dismiss such activities as nonsense. However when he visited the Island in the spring of 1977 he admitted, "I never saw anything of the kind there. Although I've known a number of houses with a disturbing atmosphere, that wasn't true of Billingham. I enjoyed the place."

He did recall that a relative told him that she "saw something" and that his son, as a very small boy, complained, "Daddy, I don't like that little woman who keeps looking at me from the dovecote...."

KING CHARLES' HEAD

Billingham made national news after the visit of Shane Leslie and his family in the late 1920s. Sir Shane, a relative of Sir Winston Churchill, friend of Tolstoy, poet, historian, author and eminent critic, wrote about his experiences in "A Ghost in the Isle of Wight", although he disguised the location of the haunted manor by calling it Killington. His first wife,

Lady Marjorie Leslie, shared these startling events and recalled them in her autobiography. Lady Leslie's haunted holiday is related in detail by Alasdair Alpin MacGregor in "The Ghost Book" (Robert Hale, 1955). In a fascinating chapter entitled "Strange happenings at Billingham Manor" he describes how she and her servants all spent their first night at the manor in a nervous state which none of them could explain. Next day two maids reported that something had been rustling about their rooms.

Haunted Billingham Manor near Chillerton - from a line drawing of 1910.

The following night Lady Leslie was woken by a commotion in the bedroom and the hall. It sounded as if furniture was being hurled around. She slammed home the bolt on her door and as she did so, there was a blow on the outside of it followed by the sound of a sword being drawn from a scabbard. Next morning not a stick of furniture was out of place, and all doors and windows were secure. Lady Leslie's puzzlement grew when the cook said she had heard footsteps in the hall that night, had called out, and had been answered by a man with a beautiful voice, "It's all right ..."

Later that week, the children's nanny had the latch of her room lifted, saw chairs she had put against the door pushed aside, and heard what seemed like the thud of a falling body; at which point the air was filled with the heavy but exquisite scent of Madonna lilies. This perfume, always associated with Billingham, was encountered by Elizabeth and Spencer Forbes and many previous owners.

The tradition that Charles I rode out to the manor from his captivity at Carisbrooke Castle but finally rejected a plan of escape devised by the loyal Worsleys, lies behind Billingham's most extraordinary story. It is recounted by Sir Shane.

He was woken by those noises in the night and decided to investigate. Followed by the whole household, he made his way downstairs. In the dining room was a corner recess covered by a sliding panel - probably a smuggler's hiding-place, since the old house, with its secret stairs and passageways lies on the smuggling route from Chale Bay; and through the cracks around this panel, light glowed in the darkness. Sir Shane pushed the panel aside. Everyone was dazzled by a sudden brightness.

"Each one of us beheld the living and severed head of His Sacred Majesty King Charles the First staring at us out of the recess. The soft ringlets, the silken and pointed beard, the regal but pitiful expression were not to be mistaken."

Sir Shane later discovered that the apparition had been seen twice before, shining out and then slowly fading away. Each time it had been on the occasion of an Island execution. He checked on the date of his own sighting. On that very morning a murderer had been hanged at Parkhurst prison.

SHE WOKE IN TERROR

A monk in a brown habit is another of Billingham's ghosts. He has been seen in the gardens. The noise of furniture or other heavy articles being moved in the middle of the night was heard by a housekeeper in 1949, exactly as the Leslies had heard it 20 years earlier.

In "The Ghost Book" it is recorded that in 1950, shortly before a sighting of the grey lady, Mr and Mrs Perks and a relative felt the house shaking violently, so violently that doors and windows rattled. This

Billingham Manor glimpsed through the front gates.

happened to the Forbes family. Spencer Forbes recalled: "The whole house has shaken, with china and pottery tinkling on the sideboard."

Then there is the scent of lilies. When it appears it pervades the hall and music room. Elizabeth Forbes last encountered it in the winter of 1974-75. It seems to be summoned by music - any kind of music. Play a pop song or a Mozart piano concerto, and a guest may well murmur, "What's that lovely smell?"

In 1962 an amused gardener asked Spencer why he had walked about the grounds in "those funny clothes." He was surprised. So was the gardener when he learned that his master had been out at the time - and certainly had not been attired in a red Georgian frock-coat.

Elizabeth stepped into the past very soon after moving into the manor. She woke in the night, and she woke in terror. Her bed was being shaken, yet she couldn't get up, couldn't even move.

"I had a terrible feeling of fear," she said. "Outside I could hear horses galloping. And then, in the room I saw two figures in 17th century costume; a man in brown and a woman in a red dress. I couldn't move to switch on a light, but the figures seemed to provide their own illumination - it was as if I was looking at a tableau or a scene on a stage. What was so awful was the way the bed was being shaken. Then gradually the figures faded away and with that the shaking stopped." Curiously, the following morning she found that her normally accurate bedside clock had lost exactly one hour.

Elizabeth and Spencer did much to restore the old house to its former state, ridding it of accretions introduced in the past. Apparently the ghosts are grateful. There have been no manifestations in recent years, report the present owners, Dr and Mrs Michael Laurence - a trifle ruefully. And if the phantoms have faded, how appropriate in this setting that they should do so after the fashion of that famous apparition of John Aubrey's which, in 1670, "disappeared with a curious perfume and most melodious twang ...."

The driveway to Billingham Manor is shown in this engraving of 1892.

Chapter Eight

THE HAUNTED HOSPITAL

For nearly 100 years the Royal National Hospital at Ventnor fought the good fight - and a long, hard fight it was - against tuberculosis. Today the killer has largely been conquered, but during the hospital's century of service some 100,000 victims of the disease sought new hope in a grey, balconied Victorian building set in lawns, woodlands and winding walks overlooking the English Channel. Many patients there were cured and discharged. Others did not leave alive. And a few, it would seem, never left at all. Their spirits remain to this day.

With the development of new drugs the old hospital, in its day among the finest in Europe numbering Queen Victoria and King Edward VII among its patrons, was itself doomed. Intimations of its mortality were first received in 1958. By 1960 the Ministry of Health announced that it would definitely close and in May 1964, its doors were padlocked. As a local landmark and very much a part of Island life, the RNH would surely have a new future, reasoned Island residents. They were wrong.

Plans became projects and then dwindled as hopes were dashed. The splendid old place would have a fresh life as a convalescent home, a school, a teachers' training college, a police cadet college. The suggestions came and went. It could be converted into flats, a holiday camp, a factory. Eventually a far-sighted Ventnor Urban District Council purchased the 33-acre site from the Ministry to turn it into botanical gardens.

Over the four years that had passed since its closure, the hospital had been left to the ravages of weather and vandals. Dilapidated and unsafe, it would have to go. Gosport demolition contractors Treloar and Sons were called in. On a sunny day in June 1969, the first bricks fell - and out of the dust came a ghost story which spread far beyond the Island.

The end of the summer brought the first headlines. "Hospital End Makes Spirit Move?" inquired the Southern Evening Echo. "Demolition Man Sees Ghost," announced the Isle of Wight Mercury. From that September until the end of the year what really happened at the Royal

National Hospital was a talking point not only on the Island, but around the globe. Ventnor, UK, made world news.

Stephen Kevern, then aged 17 and living in Ocean View Road, Ventnor, was one of the demolition men. At work in what had been the operating theatre, he found himself being watched by a "white-grey image" resembling a doctor in a hospital coat. Peter Henderson, then 19, of York Road, Upper Ventnor, twice heard the sound of a child's moans while working above the former X-ray room. Cliff Farmer, from Bonchurch, another 19-year-old, was with Peter when they both heard screams coming from a room next to the operating theatre. Tom Bryan, clerk to the local council surveyor, was reported as feeling a strange presence in the same area of the building. He told the Southern Evening Echo: "I turned to look but there was no-one there....All I can say is that I had the definite feeling that I was being watched."

No operation had been carried out in the RNH for ten years, the theatre had long been stripped of equipment and with its glass roof gone, it lay open to the elements. Yet a number of people smelled ether and the smell persisted. Mr R.Bodenham, the site agent, with 17 years in demolition work and well aware of the tricks atmosphere can play on imagination in a deserted building, summed it up. "There are things about that hospital which defy rational explanation."

THE SECRET WATCHERS

Many local people thought it all a joke. But others who had spoken to white-faced workmen and visited the site themselves did not. So it went on. Demolition men did not talk about their experiences so freely now, perhaps because they were too often ridiculed; but to listeners with open minds they could confide stories which had no rational explanation. There are always hoaxers. But hoaxers are not content with talking of vague shapes, a momentary cry, a shadow that shouldn't have been there on a sunless day - and above all a constant feeling of being watched.

Some workmen wouldn't talk at all, like the ones who in October that year saw something that was no vague shape. They were "shattered" they said, and, lighting cigarettes with shaking fingers, left it at that. It was in that month too that another contractor was reported as being "badly affected" by one of those secret watchers he could sense but never see.

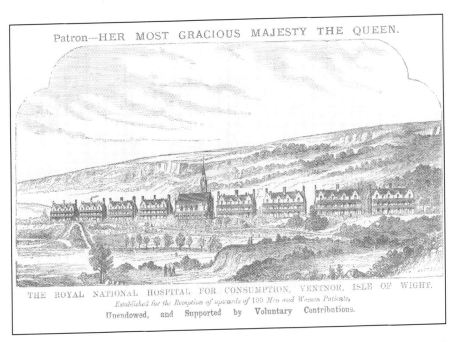

Patron—HER MOST GRACIOUS MAJESTY THE QUEEN.

THE ROYAL NATIONAL HOSPITAL FOR CONSUMPTION, VENTNOR, ISLE OF WIGHT.
Established for the Reception of upwards of 100 Men and Women Patients.
Unendowed, and Supported by Voluntary Contributions.

So disturbing became the haunting of the Royal National Hospital that in November 1969, an official report was drawn up and put into the hands of an Island clergyman. The question of exorcism was considered. The ritual was not performed, at least not by the Anglican or Roman Catholic churches, though some kind of service was held secretly on November 11, the eve of Martinmas. It may have achieved its ends, for there were few reports of any untoward incident after Christmas. By the following July, the demolition was complete.

Today there is little trace in the beautiful Ventnor Botanic Gardens of that half-mile long hospital. A variety of exotic shrubs and flowers join daffodils, violets and primroses in colouring the spring. A famous institution, ghosts and all, has gone. Perhaps with such a vigorous history, it was right not to go quietly. Perhaps some visitors are still touched by a cold shadow beneath the massive firs or find something disquieting in a quietness broken only by the incessant clack and calling of the crows.

Further stories of the haunted hospital and its long-dead patients who still roam the Botanic Gardens appear in *More Ghosts of the Isle of Wight*.

Chapter Nine

ADVENTURES IN TIME

"Time, like an ever-rolling stream, bears all its sons away ...." So says the old hymn. But is everything borne away? What is Time? What separates our Past from our Present and Future? For instance through the window of a railway carriage, a field of grazing cattle emerges from the future, becomes the present, and glides away into the past. To another observer surveying the entire scene as our train rattles by, our future, present and past are one. Is it possible that on rare occasions we see more than we should, that we break out of our limited Now? Many well-documented accounts in Proceedings of the Society for Psychical Research imply that in some sense the future can be said to be contemporaneous with the present. Is the same true of the past?

Can timeslips or timewarps occur? If so, did a Newbridge woman and a St. Helens couple at different times and places - at a lonely crossroads on an autumn evening, and high on the Downs on a starless winter night - somehow enter a different age.

PITS OF THE DEAD

It is well over half-a-century since Mildred Morris, of Newbridge, stepped back in time where Dark Lane reaches Dodpits Cross - the crossroads at the Pits of the Dead. What she saw remained impressed upon her memory. It was something she could not explain. She was a little girl making her way home from Shalfleet school that October day in 1928. She'd stayed late, being coached for an exam, the other children having left long ago. It was growing dark, though that didn't worry a country girl like her.

Mildred set off for home, wondering what mother had ready for tea. Soon she could see the distant welcome of lamplight from the cottages. At Dodpits Cross the signpost pointed her on. But as she reached the crossroads she paused. There was something wrong with that familiar signpost. Something very wrong indeed. It grew bigger and taller, its silhouette stark against the darkening sky. It was a gibbet, and swinging from it was a hanged man.

Dead eyes stared down at the staring child - and after all these years, Mildred remembers the man as if she saw him yesterday. He was shadowy but could be seen clearly enough. The head in the hempen noose had black hair that fell in long curls to the shoulders. He was bearded. He wore a cloak of some dark material, the folds of which hid his hands and arms. There is this convincing little detail: the body wore only one of its knee-high riding boots. The other lay on the ground beneath a stockinged foot.

Mildred wasn't frightened at first. In fact she was very interested. Then an evening breeze swelled the dead man's cloak and sent him swaying towards her. Fear came. In that instant, as curiosity turned to terror, the figure vanished and the signpost was a signpost once again. But she was running on and did not stop until her mother's arms were around her. When she had gasped out her story, her grandmother who had also been listening, looked thoughtful. Her grandmother, she said, had told her that up to the end of the 18th century they still hanged condemned men at that crossroads. Dark Lane had been a dark lane indeed.

TWO WHO STEPPED OUT OF TIME

At 6.30 pm on Saturday, January 4, 1969, Sheila White and her husband, a St Helens doctor, drove out of the village over the Downs and into a mystery which has never been solved. It is one of the most fascinating accounts to have come my way of a happening which cannot be fitted into the mundane scheme of things.

Sadly, both Dr White and his wife are now dead. But their intriguing and inexplicable account of that night's events holds a prime place in Isle of Wight paranormal history, and may well fit into the category of timeslip or timewarp. "Of course, at the time we were completely shattered. But I often think I would like to experience it again. It was all so very strange . . ." Sheila said later.

The couple were on their way to see friends at Niton. They had time in hand, so although it was a dark night they decided to take the road over the Downs. A high moon threw little illumination between banks of cloud as they rounded Ashey Down, but there were lights on the ground. Sheila noticed them and was puzzled. They were numerous and appeared to be flickering to and fro in the fields beside that lonely road. She drew her husband's attention to them, and they were still discussing what they might be when their car reached the top of the hill. An amazing sight spread out before them.

What they should have seen was a dark landscape through which ran the road to Mersley Down. Instead, the fields on their right were dotted with innumerable lights. They stopped the car and stared.

Millions of lights, most of them orange in colour, blazed across those empty fields and stretched as far as the sea. They could have been looking down on a city. Ahead, halfway across the Down opposite, they saw the line of the lane which leads to Havenstreet. Only it wasn't a lane that night. It was a road, illuminated by lamps on each side, and it led towards what appeared to be crowded blocks of buildings glaring with coloured lights.

Amazed, and becoming more than a little uneasy, the couple drove on. They passed the turning to Knighton Gorges and Newchurch on their left, reached the lane to Havenstreet on their right - and suddenly it was a track again. Beyond, the fields were dark once more. It was as if someone had flicked down a switch on that landscape of lights. The whole astonishing scene had gone.

Sheila remembers that they stopped the car and got out for a while, trying to make sense of it all and failing. "My husband as a doctor, was a far from credulous person. He was furious we couldn't explain it," she recalled. He told her, "I am glad you saw it too - I thought I was going mad".

When the lights disappeared the familiar Island countryside became suddenly threatening. The darkness weighed upon the couple and there was something vaguely unreal about clouds that were like a range of black mountains, something sinister about that shining moon. "A great depression came upon me," recalled Sheila. "I wanted to burst into tears."

They resumed their journey. Ahead lay the Hare and Hounds inn where over a stiff brandy they might attempt to account for what they had seen. Logic, reason, commonsense would prevail. There must be an answer, if only they could think of it. But before they reached the Hare and Hounds they had another bizarre encounter.

As they took the last bend in the road on Gallows Hill the inn came into brilliant sight. It seemed to be floodlit. Everywhere lights had blazed into life again. To the right the fields were shimmering as they had been on Mersley Down, in front of them a carpet of light was unrolled towards Newport. To and fro across the road, ran figures who bore flaring torches. There were about a hundred of them. Sheila remembered one particularly well. It was the figure of a man, an unusually tall man wearing a long jerkin and a wide leather belt.

"He had a very handsome profile," she recalled with a smile. How did she notice him among so many? "He literally passed through the bonnet of the car. Right through it. Then he vanished."

When they reached the Hare and Hounds, lights and figures disappeared, suddenly and completely. Again, utterly bewildered, they stopped the car. The pub windows shed a welcome in the darkness. That was all. Their headlights picked out nothing but road, verge and hedgerow. Around them, shadowy fields stretched out into blackness. Through an ordinary winter night they drove on, with nothing more to disturb them and a seemingly incredible story to tell.

Sheila told that story quietly and thoughtfully. The only time a certain asperity crept into her tone was when people offered explanations of the more fatuous kind. "A farmers' barbecue...the eyes of sheep reflected in our headlights ...glow-worms! Really!"

For years afterwards she asked herself whether it was just a mirage, some trick of the light that reflected the mainland scene and lights from Portsmouth. But what about those figures, the man in the jerkin? Perhaps on that January night she and her husband were allowed to stand back far enough from Time to see both the future and the past.

Did they see stretching northwards from Mersley Down a future Island suburb of some vast Solent city? Did she see on Gallows Hill torchbearers of the Roman Legions long ago?

Chapter Ten

WAGERS WITH DEATH

A MURDERED MINSTREL

A murdered minstrel, a drowned trooper, portraits that could carry a curse, ghostly footsteps that echoed miles away in a Newport newspaper office - these are the ingredients of the strange story of Wolverton Manor. Incredible, of course; except that those footsteps have been heard by owner after owner at the manor and by cynical journalists inclined to scoff at the supernatural.

The Elizabethan mansion lies about half a mile from Shorwell. There has been a building on the site since the days of Edward the Confessor, but the manor-house was built by a descendant of the Dingleys who came to the Island in the reign of Richard II.

When the unfortunate minstrel met his death there is unknown. His excellence was his undoing. He fiddled so well that he was well rewarded, and servants, greedy for gold, killed him as he slept. Hence the manor's haunted room.

The unlucky trooper came later, foolishly headed his horse across the Withy Bed swamp behind the house, and was swallowed up. A bedroom looks over what is now known as Trooper's Wood and this room, too, seems to be a favourite haunt.

Footsteps, whether of fiddler or trooper, have been heard at Wolverton for centuries. People living there became accustomed to the invisible walker who shuffled along the landings and down the stairs. They grew used to that unseen walker opening their door and strolling around their bed.

He walked in the hall, too, where household dogs showed every sign of actually seeing him. Building work or alterations seemed to disturb the ghost. He would walk more often and, a curious touch, in the mornings the occupants would find that the carpets in the hall had their edges turned up.

Although the Patterson family, who bought Wolverton in 1972, are still doing a considerable amount of renovation work on the ancient building, nothing strange has occurred lately. "All is quiet," they said.

Haunted Wolverton Manor, Shorwell, photographed in 1910.

A TRAGIC LOVE STORY

Now for a fascinating link with the former offices of the Southern Evening Echo. Though modernised and converted into a shop, this old building in Newport High Street is thought to have originally formed part of a town house owned by John Phillips, 17th century owner of Span Manor, in the parish of Godshill. His daughter, Henrietta, born in 1685, spent much of her time in that house. There she met and fell in love with Phillip Colenet, grandson of Sir Robert Dillington of Knighton Gorges.

One day Henrietta was taken gravely ill while he was away from town. When he heard the news, the young man saddled the fleetest horse in his stables and rode to Newport as he had never ridden before; but she died before he could reach her on Midsummer's Day, 1703. It is recorded that the year after Henrietta's death, Phillip Colenet bought the house from her father and lived there like a recluse until he died 22 years later.

Portraits of the two lovers hang at Wolverton Manor. They were sold after Phillip's death to the Delgarno family who owned the manor

Portraits of the two lovers still hang today at Wolverton Manor.

in the early 18th century. The legend that a curse will fall upon anyone who moves them is well known. Wolverton's owners change. The portraits stay. Is it through them that something out of the manor's haunted history has found its way to the former newspaper offices in that Newport street? Again, it is the sound of footsteps.

"They gave me goose-pimples," admitted former Echo reporter Maurice Leppard. "I was working late one night and I heard them absolutely clearly going across the floor of the empty room above me. A moment earlier there had been a curious shuddering noise in the blocked-up chimney-breast. Then the footsteps. I looked up, half-expecting to see something coming through the ceiling."

When he checked that empty room he was even more puzzled. Who could walk heavily across a floor covered with boxes and stacks of old newspapers? Maurice was one of several Echo newsmen to hear the phantom footsteps.

Other people working there also knew of the midnight walker who climbed a now vanished staircase and passed through walled-up doors. But an hour or so before they heard him, did a door silently open, miles away in an ancient manor? Does something still stir in the Withy Bed swamp?

The old Echo offices with their battered typewriters, dusty piles of copy and heaps of old newspapers are now a thing of the past, an anachronism in these days of high-tech computers and modern methods of news gathering. The old house where Philip Colenet lived out his lonely days has been transformed into a bright and welcoming women's fashion shop.

Does the ghost still walk there? Yes, according to staff who report odd noises coming from that upstairs room when no customers are about. Doors open by themselves and what sounds like footsteps cross the now carpeted floor overhead. "We don't mind. We just look at one another and say, 'The ghost is walking again'," they smiled.

WAGER WITH DEATH

Tragedy was certainly nothing new for the Dillington family, which finally died out in 1721 when Sir Tristram, last of the line, committed suicide. His body was found floating in the lake at Knighton Gorges on July 14 and his ghost has since been seen driving a coach and four on the anniversary of his death. Sir Tristram Dillington, uncle to the unfortunate Phillip Colenet, was a reckless gambler, who on the day he died, had lost his Newport town house on the turn of a card. The luckless knight, gaming with noblemen friends at Seal House in Sea Street (then named Shispoole Street), wagered the property in a game of cards. His gamble cost him

Seal House, Newport.

dear. On the turn of a low card Sir Tristram lost the house and all it contained to Mr John Redstone.

Curiously, Seal House has its own ghost - a little ginger-haired apparition which knelt at the end of a bed, grinning. It made such an impression on a young Newport girl, that forty years later she could still

Seal House, Newport, from a nineteeth century engraving.

picture him clearly. At the time, Joy Adsett and her family were living in the large three-storey house, built in 1697, which overlooks Newport Quay. "I could only have been about five at the time, and when I saw that face appear at the end of the bed, I screamed for my mum and dad. They came rushing up the spiral staircase, but by that time, the apparition with the impish grin had faded and I never saw him again," said Joy.

The family later moved a few doors away to an old cottage, Number 24 Sea Street, which has now been demolished and replaced by a council car park. Then one day Joy's grandmother, the splendidly named Queenie Victoria Eggerton, arrived to stay for a few days.

She was made welcome by the family and duly installed in her room. However Queenie did not sleep well that night - in fact she hardly slept at all. "When we got up the next morning, there was Nan, sitting downstairs with all her bags packed ready to leave," said Joy.

"She told us that the ghost of a little old lady in queer, old-fashioned black clothes had been standing in the corner of the bedroom all night, watching her. Nan was so unnerved by this that she refused to stay another night and although she would come for the day, she never slept in that house again!"

Chapter Eleven

MURDERERS AND THE MURDERED

THE DEADLY AXE

Resentment smouldered. His grandson was young and handsome and had come into money; while he grew old, bent-backed, as he swung his axe against oak and elm, which fell to bring gold to his master but only coppers to him. One sullen day he dragged himself back to his cottage to find the boy was late with his meal. It was enough. He cursed, took his axe from his shoulder and a blade sharp enough to cut through to heartwood bit into flesh and bone. Blood oozed into the earth floor. Blood stained the walls and the flagstones round the fire.

Desperately he threw brushwood on that fire until the flames licked the ceiling, burning their way through lath and plaster while the thatch above whispered and crackled under a cloud of smoke. Perhaps the falling roof would burn the body and blacken the red stone. Perhaps he would be left to weep, unsuspected, for a dead boy and a lost home.

But he had brooded too openly or said too much over his ale. It may be that the gashed body told too obvious a story when charred timbers were hauled away. The magistrates called in the military. A manhunt began. It was not long before a haggard, starving fugitive was dragged from a cave not far from the scene of his crime. He was tried at Winchester Assizes, sentenced to death, and hanged. His body was brought back to the Island, coated in pitch and displayed in a corpse-cage on the public gibbet at Downend.

This is the popular and best-known version of the story of Michal (or Micah) Morey, the murderous woodcutter, and the tale of his dark deed has become part of Island folklore - as well it might. But as the story has been handed down through the years, fact and fiction have been distorted and blurred.

There is no question that Morey did exist and that his crime was even nastier than the accepted account would have us believe. According to researcher Kenneth Phillips in his book "For Rooks and Ravens", Michal Morey killed 14-year-old James Dove in cold blood. An account of the trial at Winchester Assizes on 19th March, 1737, revealed:

The Hare and Hounds at Downend, Arreton.

"An old fellow of the Isle of Wight was condemned for the murder of his grandson, about 14 years of age. He had bred him up from the cradle; and the child having some way disobliged him he took him out with him one morning about six o'clock in June last, on the pretence of going to a market town to buy necessaries and carried him into a wood and murdered him with a billhook which he had taken with him for that purpose. He had cut off his head and mangled his body, and put the whole into two wallets which he also carried with him..."

Morey lay low for a week. When he returned home without the boy, neighbours became suspicious and a search of his belongings revealed a bloody shirt. Whatever house was burnt in Burnt House Lane, it was not Michal Morey's.

The dark deed was committed in June, but the boy's remains lay undiscovered until October, when the long hot summer had done its work. Two large leather bags were found in woods to the west of Arreton. The stained and rusty billhook was still recognisable. The dismembered, putrefying body was not. Only the boy's hat, breeches, stocking and shoes could be identified. His pathetic remains were finally laid to rest in Arreton Churchyard.

The Public Bar of the Hare and Hounds showing the old beam said to be part of the gibbet, from a photograph taken in the 1940s.

During his brief trial, Michal Morey made little attempt to explain himself or confess. Sentence was passed and he was hanged within the hour. If ever a ghost walked, his should. And of course it does. You may meet it, deadly axe on shoulder, trudging down Burnt House Lane, which runs between Newport and Downend. It walks, too in the general area of Gallows Hill near the Hare and Hounds inn, where you can see among the rafters the supposed crossbeam of the old gibbet with a notch cut in it beside the date of his execution. The skull on show there is not the murderer's however.

Although once exhibited to Queen Victoria, it was exhumed by men digging in an ancient tumulus on the Down in 1878 and belongs to a much more ancient skeleton.

This skull was on display in the bar.

One old Islander who saw Morey's ghost recalled, "I was cycling along Burnt House Lane one night just after the last war. It was moonlight and the road was clear, so I was surprised when I suddenly saw a man walking towards me near the lane that leads to Great East Standen. He hadn't been there the moment before. I thought he must have stepped out of the hedgerow. When I got closer I could see he was wearing some sort of leather leggings and a leather jerkin but the rest of his clothes were ragged. The oddest thing was his hat, a floppy black thing with a feather or two tucked in it. I thought he had a shotgun over his shoulder but when I reached him I saw it was a big axe with a piece of cloth tied round the blade. I glanced back the second I'd passed him, he looked so odd - but he'd gone. I couldn't believe he'd just vanished. It wasn't possible. That old bike fair shook, the speed I pedalled back to Newport ..."

GREAT DARK SOCKETS

Michal Morey's corpse was left rotting on the Downend gibbet until it became, even in that desolate spot, an offence to eye and nostril. Villagers from Arreton petitioned for its removal. Their request was granted and the remains were buried in an unmarked grave. It was, of course, common for bodies of murderers and suicides to he buried at crossroads, and it was at the crossroads, formed by roads and a footpath at the Arreton turn, half a mile south of Gallows Hill that a holidaymaker saw a fearful sight late one September night in 1974.

Elizabeth Leverson, of Trinity Road, London, SW14, had been visiting friends at Staplers, Newport. Driving back to her Sandown hotel she had to brake sharply at the turn to Arreton when another vehicle took the corner wide. Her car stalled for a moment and as she was starting again she noticed in her wing mirror a strange-looking figure standing motionless on the right hand side of the road; so strange a figure that she glanced back through her window.

"There was enough moonlight for me to be sure of what I saw," she said. "I'm never likely to forget it. It was the figure of a man dressed in a sort of greyish-coloured smock with a wide belt round the middle. His arms were twisted behind him as if they were tied to this belt at the back. But what was so horrible was his head. It was lolling on one side and there were holes where eyes should have been - great dark sockets

- and shreds of something hanging down his mouth and cheeks. I felt sick. I closed my eyes for a second, and thank heavens, when I opened them again he'd gone."

THE WAXWORKS PHANTOM

From a murderer to the murdered. Echoes of a Victorian murder in Nodgham Lane, Carisbrooke, are still felt, as for many years local people have complained of a pain in the back as they pass the spot where a girl was stabbed. The garden of a house in Watergate Road, Newport, is said to be haunted by the ghost of an over-zealous Puritan who spat at King Charles I on his way to Carisbrooke Castle and was promptly thrown down his own well by Royalists.

A popular Isle of Wight tourist attraction boasts the ghost of a murdered Frenchman, the unfortunate Louis de Rochefort whose forlorn phantom haunts the timber-framed, early Tudor building at Brading, now the Isle of Wight Wax Works. The museum first opened in the early 1960s when two ancient character cottages were knocked into one. Dating back to 1499 AD, these tiny dwellings served over the centuries as a Guild house, brew house and coaching inn known as The Crown. Brading was formerly an important harbour and Wall Lane was known as Quay Lane until the harbour was drained in 1888.

De Rochefort who is thought to have to have been a French agent sent to make contact with the imprisoned King Charles at Carisbrooke Castle, stabled his horse and took lodgings at The Crown. He never left. He was foully murdered by unknown (but probably Puritan) hands and tradition has it that with his dying breath he vowed to haunt the building until his body was returned to France. He appears, literally, to keep his word. The ghost of a tall, thin, strangely-dressed man has been sighted many times wandering about the cottage garden and it is said that animals, particularly dogs, grow disturbed at the spot on the first floor where he was killed.

In 1964, workmen digging a water main at the ancient Elizabeth Cottages unearthed the skeleton of a man and there was speculation that it might be that of de Rochefort after experts dated the bones to the 17th century. Attempts were made to trace his birthplace or descendants so that the remains could be returned and the haunting ended. They were unsuccessful. As Graham Osborn-Smith, whose family formerly owned the museum, put it in his guide book, "His ghost may well be doomed to restlessly pervade the confines of these ancient walls until the end of time..."

The Isle of Wight Wax Works where the ghost of a murdered Frenchman still walks.

And it seems that Louis may not be the only unquiet spirit there. In the 1950s the last tenant left in a hurry after hearing voices arguing in the night and the sound of running water where there was none. Members of the Carley family, whose home it was for over 100 years, told of jumping in haste from their beds to try and catch a glimpse of the coach and four that often woke them as it clattered down Quay Lane at dead of night.

GHOST CHILDREN OF BRADING

The boy came first. Aged nine or ten, he wore patched, threadbare trousers which were cut off at the knees. His name, he said, was Sully. His companion, Rosa, a pale faced little ragamuffin in a torn frock, appeared a month or so later. Both were ghosts.

They haunted a small terraced house in Brading, just across the High Street from the Isle of Wight Wax Works, where they were seen by young Martin Dexter. The old house was the home of Ann, his elder sister, who takes up the story.

"When Martin was about four, he stayed with me two or three nights a week in the early 1990s. He came downstairs one day and demanded to know 'Why won't that little boy play with me?'

"When I asked what he was on about, Martin pointed to the staircase and told me there was a little boy sitting on the stairs. I could see nothing and thought he was making it up; that he had invented an imaginary friend or play-mate," Ann said.

But Martin insisted that the other boy really was there, and over the next few weeks came out with some startling details. Ann admitted, "I was was quite spooked by it. I never saw or felt anything myself, but I really think Martin did. He told me, 'The little boy stands there and watches but he won't play with me'."

Another time Martin came downstairs and said that the boy's name was Sully, that he looked ever so white, and spoke without moving his mouth. On this occasion he was accompanied by a girl called Rosa. She never joined in with Martin's games, but would just sit with Sully and watch. For the next 18 months the pair would appear in the back bedroom and Martin would sometimes tell Ann of their visits.

"Apparently Sully used to live in that house a long time ago when, as he put it, the house had hair on the roof. In those days, according to the little ghost, the Island's roads were just made of dirt and there were horses and carts in the street outside."

One day four-year-old Martin announced, "Sully told me how he died. He was in a fire. The window was in the roof and he tried to shout out for help, but the people in the street didn't hear him."

"After that I was convinced Martin wasn't making it up and I was really quite glad to leave the house a few months later," said Ann. But by this time Martin and Sully were firm friends and they stayed in touch. One night Martin was at his grandmother's house in Station Road, Brading. He was in bed and she heard him whispering, "Sully, go home, go home. You don't live here. Go home."

"Mum said it made her flesh creep," shivered Ann.

So, were Sully and Rosa simply two imaginary playmates dreamed up by a young boy? Or were they two little spirits who belonged to another time..... when those ancient cottages in Brading High Street had thatched roofs?

END

INDEX

NOT SPOOKED YET? WHY NOT ORDER
YOUR PERSONAL, AUTOGRAPHED COPIES
OF THE ORIGINAL GHOSTS OF THE ISLE OF WIGHT
MORE GHOSTS OF THE ISLE OF WIGHT
GHOSTS OF THE ISLE OF WIGHT III
AND ISLE OF WIGHT GHOSTS BOOK IV
(They also make thoughtful gifts for nervous friends)

Send this order form with your name and address to:

Gay Baldwin
9 Pine Tree Close
Cowes
Isle of Wight
PO31 8DX
Telephone (01983 294651)

.... copies of Ghosts of the IW   @ £3.95 each   £.............

.... copies of More Ghosts of the IW   @ £4.95 each   £.............

.... copies of Ghosts of the IW book III @ £6.95 each   £.............

.... copies of Ghosts of the IW book IV @ £6.95 each   £.............

Add 75p postage and packing for the first book and 50p for each
additional book.

                                                          £.............

                                        TOTAL   £.............

NOTE: We usually dispatch orders the same or next day. Please allow
two weeks before you panic. If a book has to be somewhere by a certain
date, let us know so we can try to get it there on time.